Walking on Sunshine

Sixteen Years of Love
to a Divine Transformation

(3rd edition)

Walking on Sunshine

Sixteen Years of Love
to a Divine Transformation
(3rd Edition)

Sheryl Hill

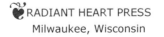
RADIANT HEART PRESS
Milwaukee, Wisconsin

Lyrics to *Ooh Aah* by GRITS.
Writer Credits: Teron Carter / Stacey Jones / Toby Mckeehan / Otto Price / Rick Robbins,
Copyright: © 2002 Universal Music – Brentwood Benson Songs (BMI) / COF Music (BMI) / Five
E Music (BMI). All rights for the world on behalf of COF Music & Five E Music administered by
Universal Music—Brentwood Benson Songs / Achtober Songs (BMI) / Twelve Eighteen Music
(BMI) / Butter Hits Music (BMI). All Rights Reserved. Used By Permission.

Lyrics to *Walking on Sunshine*, by Katrina and the Waves,
recorded 1985, permission requested.

Photos from Dr. Matsuro Emoto used with permission.

Published by
Radiant Heart Press
An imprint of HenschelHAUS Publishing, Inc.
2625 S. Greeley St. Suite 201
Milwaukee, WI 53207
www.henschelHAUSbooks.com
Please contact the publisher for quantity discounts.

ISBN: 978159598-204-9
LCCN: 2012948614
e-ISBN: 978159598-205-6

Library of Congress Cataloging-in-Publication Data
available on request.

Cover design by EM Graphics.

Originally published by XLibris under
ISBN: 978-1-4568-2513-3

Printed in the United States of America.

Proceeds from the sale of this book benefit DepartSmart.org,
a 501 (c) (3) non-profit. Purchase is tax deductible
to the extent allowable by the Internal Revenue Service.

For the AHs in my life:

Allen Hill and Alec Hill

Table of Contents

Preface i

Death is Not a Stranger 1

God Called My Name 6

Sweet Boy 8

Badge of Courage 10

Being Normal 12

Tonsil Ick To Me 18

Blessings Are To Be Shared 20

Until Japan 24

Every Ending is a New Beginning 26

Four to Six Weeks 40

Mountainous Fontaine 52

Dragonflies and Indigo 55

The Spirit Book 61

Becoming One 65

Angelic Anniversary 72

The Purplest 76

Eleven-Eleven 79

Brothers 86

DNA... 93

Retinitis Pigmentosa 95

Raging Grief 101

Table of Contents, *continued*

Spirit Healing.. 104
An Angry God 107
Habakkuk and Malachi 112
Holy Water.. 118
Into the Dark 125
Sweet as Honey... 136
Anger Zaps.. 139
Tyler Evidence.. 145
Merkabah 151
Love Eye in Heaven.. 161
Sun Signals 172
Wonder 181
YeM!.. 185
Afterword.. 187

References & Resources 191

About the Author 193

About Depart Smart 195

Preface

Heaven called my sixteen-year-old son, Tyler Hill, home in 2007. His story is one of life after death, evidence that love never dies, that energy (NRG) cannot be created or destroyed, only transformed. Tyler lives in the light of eternal love. His love and glorious soul are ever present. He lived fully with diabetes, traveling, loved well, and enjoyed his short time here on earth.

In Tyler's science notebook, he repeatedly abbreviated "energy" as NRG. One quote by Albert Einstein Tyler had written stood out in particular: "NRG cannot be created. It can only be changed from one form to another."

After Tyler's death, karma ran over my dogma. As I began to chronicle this collection of vignettes about Tyler's life, that of my family, and other dear ones who have transitioned. I held this promise close to my heart: "I did not lose the ones I love who passed away. They are transformed!"

Dr. Lerma, author of *Into the Light*, wrote of pre-death experiences in palliative care. His book describes the souls of dying and deceased patients reaching out to loved ones. Many of Dr. Lerma's dying patients spoke of an iridescent rainbow that filled the room with a sphere as bright as the sun beneath it. I have a photo of this phenomenon, which I talk about later in this book. Dr. Lerma encouraged me to tell, to publish, and to bring hope to mothers, fathers, brothers, sisters, friends, family, community, and nations who grieve for loved ones who have passed away.

Since *Walking on Sunshine: NRG—A Divine Transformation* was first published, I have met so many others who have received signs of love and promise from their "dearly departed." It's as if we need permission to speak about something so awesomely healing.

Be blessed. Be the blessing.

Sheryl Hill
Mound, Minnesota
2017

Death is Not a Stranger

I was vomiting profusely, unable to keep anything down. Sleep wasn't coming too peacefully either. It was 1990. My six-year-old nephew, Joshua, had just been killed in a drunken-driver accident in Alaska, where he and his family lived. Joshie's brother, Matt, was critically injured. His mother, Sherry, would likely not survive and was in a deep coma. Joshie's two sisters, Christina and Amber, were shaken, badly bruised, heartbroken, but alive. His dad and my brother, Carl, was visiting us in Minnesota. After we heard of the tragedy, Carl, my husband, Allen, and I arrived as quickly as possible.

Joshie had lived and died in Alaska. It was a long flight from Minnesota. I had spent 18 years of my life in Alaska. Coming home to bury a kindergartner was overwhelming.

We attended Joshua's funeral. His mom was still suffering extremely severe brain trauma at the hospital. She could not be present. I held a rose that Josh's kindergarten class gave to the family after singing, *Yes, Jesus Loves Me*, at his funeral. Life was hard.

My mother embraced me in a motherly hug that I interpreted as support for grief-stricken hearts, until she whispered, "You'd better go buy a pregnancy test and be certain it isn't that." Mothers know stuff. She was right.

I nearly fainted when the plus sign appeared. One life taken away; a new one begins. It was not the beginning I had imagined or hoped for.

Sherry, Joshie's mother, my dear friend and sister-in-law, died a few weeks after Joshie. We attended her funeral—more vomiting, tears, and angst. Sherry's favorite song was *El Shaddai*, which means God Almighty. A soloist blessed us and her by singing that song at her funeral.

I was angry. My dad had died two short years before from lung cancer. The first time I saw my dad, after I heard the word terminal, I said through sobs, "Dad, are you going to die?"

He answered in his typical, matter-of-fact way, "Yes, dear, and so are you. But I am not dead yet." He was two years older than I am today. Then Joshie died. And then Sherry died.

Happier Times

The Christmas before Sherry passed, I was shopping for holiday gifts for Sherry and her family. I kept picking up a green satin pantsuit with rhinestone buttons. It was on sale, but still too pricey. I'd put it back on the rack only to regret leaving it, turn around, and go pick it up again. I did this a number of times. The saleswoman said, "You're apparently supposed to buy that outfit."

I answered, "Yes. I feel that, but my sister-in-law lives in Kenai, Alaska. I can't imagine anywhere that she would wear it."

"Well, it's marked down, and she can always mail it back for a return if you keep the receipt." That cinched the deal. I bought it, wrapped it in birthday and holiday paper, and sent it with other gifts.

One day, I picked up the phone to see if Sherry had received the packages. In Alaska, she had picked up the phone to call me. I heard the *beep beep* of numbers being pressed until she said, "Sheryl? Hello?" She was crying.

We would often call each other, me in Minnesota and her in Alaska, to catch the other one doing the same thing at the same time. Love does stuff like that.

Sherry told me that she had been feeling really blue. Sherry is not the feel-blue type—she was effervescent, generous, somewhat shy in new situations, humble, but rarely blue. I asked her why. She told me that she was so blessed and could not understand why she was being so emotional. She explained that the ladies in her church choir were singing for the senior citizens home and decided to wear sparkly holiday outfits. Sherry made most of her own clothes and clothes for her four kids. She was strapped financially, trying to make ends meet, but still generous enough to bake bread and cookies for the paramedics at the local community hospital and sing cheerfully for elderly Alaskans.

I told Sherry that the Lord works in mysterious ways and to go open the present wrapped in birthday and holiday paper. She told me, "But it's not my birthday." I told her to open it anyway, that today was her day.

She must have forgotten that I was on the telephone. I waited and waited and suddenly heard happy, chirpy laughter.

Finally, she spoke to me, "Sorry! I was so excited I had to try it on. I forgot you were holding. I love it, Sheryl! It's perfect! How did you know?"

I didn't know, but the source of love greater than us did. It was a fine miracle present. Sherry was so happy.

Sherry's Visit

At the time of Sherry's funeral, I was living in Minnesota, working for a Baby Bell telephone company in wide-area communications. I was finishing some intense training to become certified in voice, video, and data communications. I went to classes in Colorado two weeks on, one week off, for months.

After Sherry and Joshie's passing, my brother Carl and his kids, Matt, Christina, and Amber moved to Minnesota. Our mom put her life on hold to be the woman of the house for Carl and her remaining three Smith grandkids. I tried to be available and supportive as much as possible, finding a home to rent, furniture, school registrations, sponsoring a kid's play, and other such things whenever I was around.

I was angry, too. Angry that God would allow such a tragedy. The drunken driver walked away from the accident unharmed. He was sentenced to seven short years for the death of Joshua and Sherry. It hardly seemed fair. The bar that served the drunken driver was held liable. They lost their right to do business in the community.

Sherry's Alaskan pastor checked in with me often. He asked me why I was so angry. We talked about the driver and the bar. He asked me to forgive. I said, "I have, but they are not excused."

I believe in forgiveness. I also believe in justice and restitution. It's not enough to say "I'm sorry." "I'm sorry" changes nothing except maybe your ability to move on. You must right the wrong. It takes at least ten loves to remove one hurt. Tyler taught me that.

I also told the pastor that I prayed and prayed for Sherry to be whole again, and she died. His response was that Sherry was more whole today than she had ever been in her body on earth. I told him that I think God would have known what I meant. The pastor told me he would pray for me. I replied, "Great, you do that."

Many people were telling me that my mom and I had to be mothers to Amber, Chrissy, and Matt. I said, "No. I'm not. I'm going to be their auntie. No one, not anyone, can take their mom's place."

One night, I was lying in bed, worrying, thinking hard, having a conversation with Sherry in my mind. "Sister, what can I do? How can I help? You are supposed to be here! I miss you so much!"

A bright light appeared to the left of the bed a few feet away. The light had a shape similar to Sherry, with an outline of hair just above the shoulders, appearing to blow as if a breeze were in the room. A long robe of light billowed around her.

I heard her speak simple, but very Sherry words to me. "We have a great God, Sheryl. It isn't you. Let go. Trust." I hadn't taken a breath while she was speaking, and gasped when the light went away, awestruck.

God Called My Name

My firstborn son, Tyler, was born on the anniversary of D-day, June 6, 1991. He weighed in at ten pounds, two ounces. It's not always good to have big babies. Macrosomia often occurs with gestational diabetes, and stress is often a culprit. Ty was one of these babies. He had to have a glucose infusion shortly after birth. He was in intensive care for the glucose infusion when newborn pneumonia was diagnosed. Ty would not come home for two long weeks.

When he did come home, we had a great celebration with Joshie's dad, siblings, my mom, and in-laws. A new life is great fun. Four years later, I would have a second son, Alec. Ty prayed for a baby sister, but he fell in love with Alec at first sight. He was a very proud and dutiful big brother, volunteering to help diaper Alec even though it wasn't pleasant. I asked him why he wanted to do that. He replied, "Because, Mommy, I love my brother, too!"

I quit my stressful Baby Bell job and took a different track with a production company creating three-dimensional health-care videos for medical education back before Pixar was a household name.

My company was working on a diabetes information video with prominent insulin manufacturers and health-care providers. I recall how

Sheryl Hill

fortunate I felt that no one whom I loved was affected by diabetes. No potential for blindness, amputations, heart disease, or premature death.

I awoke one evening after midnight to Ty's moaning. He was in his room. I entered to find him sitting up with his arms outstretched. His eyes looked like those of a deer caught in the headlights. I held his shoulders, gave him a gentle shake, and called out, "Ty, Tyler! Wake up, Buddy. You're having a nightmare."

He opened his eyes, looking at me with tears. "Why am I here, Mommy? Why did you bring me back here? God called my name. Not the name you call me, but my real name in Heaven. Let me go, Mommy. I want to go back to Heaven."

I said, "No, Buddy. You need to stay here with me. Mommy and Daddy love you, and we need you with us. It was just a dream."

"No, Mommy. It was real. You and Daddy can't come. You can come later. Don't worry."

What can a mother do? I tucked him back into bed and tickled his back until I heard his soft sleep breathing.

Then I sobbed and prayed by the bed. "Dear God! Please don't take my son." I prayed and sobbed for hours. Exhausted, I gave up. "Dear God. If you take my son, I beg you, please give me strength."

Ty never told me his Heavenly name. He couldn't say it. He could only feel it.

Sweet Boy

Over the next few months, Ty started losing his appetite. He had low energy. He started wetting the bed and vomiting unexplainably.

On his fifth birthday, an au pair from South Africa, named Gilly, joined our family. She noticed that Ty was urinating and drinking an awful lot. I knew what I knew. I took an immediate trip to the pediatrician, who was reluctant to make a diagnosis, but informed me that Ty had sugar in his urine. So I asked the dreaded diabetes question.

The response came, "It could be worse. It's not cancer. He can live a long life with diabetes."

Ty's pediatrician called in an emergency screening at the diabetes center. I called Allen, my husband, and asked him to meet us there.

Ty looked up at me and said, "Don't cry, Mommy. I'm fine."

I told him, "Honey, life as we know it is over. Things are going to change now. It will not be a fun change."

At the diabetes center, they confirmed type 1 insulin-dependent diabetes, also known as juvenile diabetes back then. The nurse cried with us. We were required to poke Ty's finger for blood sugar tests and inject saline into his buttocks before we could take him home, only to return for the next five days for intensive education on diabetes management.

I couldn't inject. Neither could Allen. The thought of piercing our little boy's delicate skin with a sharp needle was too awful. We were anxious, stressed, and tearful.

It was Ty who said, "C'mon, Mommy. C'mon, Daddy. I want to go home. You can do it. I believe you can do it." We did it for him. He was so brave. We performed to the medical staff's satisfaction and were sent on our way.

Once outside, however, Ty locked down. He would not budge. He sat down on the sidewalk. He looked up at us under the blue sky, squinting against the sun, pointing his finger at us, and said, "You listen to me! God does not want me to have stupid diabetes. He wants me to have normal diabetes. I am not supposed to have to take two shots and live a stupid life." (Ouch.)

I told him, "Yes, baby. I know. You are and will always be my sweet boy."

Badge of Courage

True Life

It's tough being different. Ty was ostracized by first-grade classmates who teased him for being a sissy because he wore a medical alert diabetes bracelet. I submitted the following story to *Children with Diabetes* the same year:

> *I was puzzled and perplexed at the extraordinary admiration and love in the twinkling brown eyes of my six-year-old son, Tyler. He sat beside me on the school bus home, arm extended high over his head, resting on my shoulder. "Mom, I am so proud of you! You made it! You're a teacher!"*
>
> *I pulled him close to me and kissed his forehead, "Thanks, Buddy!"*
>
> *I take time off from my job for a half day each week to be a parent helper in his first-grade class. To him, I had arrived at the top. He was proud of me. He did his best work on the days I participated. I chuckled at his competent, responsible and proud behaviors.*
>
> *One day, I came to school, joyfully looking forward to cutting little black wheels for 23 bright yellow cardboard school buses. I found him curled in a corner sobbing miserably. He would not look at me. He would not talk to me. He was ashamed.*

Mrs. Anderly, his teacher, sat on the floor next to him, embraced him and waited. Slowly, patiently she gained his trust. He sobbed into her chest, sighed and told her, "The other boys in the class do not want me in their group because I wear a sissy bracelet." I saw the pain in her eyes and felt it in my heart.

A few days later, the school nurse came to his class. (Ty had asked me not to come.) All of his little classmates sat on the floor while she talked to them about health conditions.

"We all have something," she said. "If I say something that you have, raise your hand. Glasses. Allergies. Asthma. Diabetes. Fillings or cavities. Can you think of anything else? Sometimes, if we have a special health condition, we wear a medical alert bracelet to tell people how to help us. Does anyone here have one? Tyler, will you come up front and show the class."

He walked forward, eyes to the floor.

The nurse said, "Tyler wears a medical alert bracelet because he has diabetes. It can save his life."

Tyler suddenly became brave. He saw a lancet on the desk. He started telling the class about his diabetes. He held the lancet out to the class, poked his finger defiantly, squeezed a huge drop of blood out and held it before the class. Then, he took a syringe, told the class how he used it and held it up high for the whole class to see. The class was astonished!

Tyler looked at them with understanding and said, "This is not a sissy bracelet. This is my badge of courage."

"Congratulations, Buddy. I am so proud of you! You made it! You are a teacher!"

Being Normal

People without a clue would see us testing Ty's blood and say, "Oh, is he diabetic?"

Ty would respond, "No, I'm just a little boy."

When we label, we disable.

Diabetic refers to a condition of the disease, not the person: diabetic retinopathy, diabetic neuropathy, and so on. People with cancer should not be defined as cancerous. People with epilepsy should not be defined epileptic. People with asthma should not be defined asthmatic. It's offensive—diabetic should not define people. It's not nice to call people names.

We did live a stupid diabetes life for about a year. Ty took two shots of insulin a day. We chased his insulin with regimented food prescribed at precise intervals. Ty could not exercise when his long-acting insulin was peaking, or he would have a low blood sugar reaction unless he carbed up. He could not overeat at prescheduled meal times or risk a high blood sugar reaction; supplemental insulin was not offered.

He had to eat even if his little body was sick. He could not eat birthday cake and hot dogs and soda with his friends at parties. Technically, he could, but it would have to be a minuscule portion.

Being Normal

He was rail thin and gray. Despite our best efforts, his blood sugar numbers weren't all that great. A quarterly diabetes health check called an HbA1c told the story. I recall asking one of the medical professionals how long Ty would have before diabetes would take its toll. The reply was devastating: if he kept very tight control of his blood sugars, perhaps fifteen years. I was preparing for the fight of my life for Tyler.

One evening, I went to tuck Ty into bed.

He told me, "I am sick and tired of this stupid diabetes life. I want to be a normal little boy. I don't mind the shots, Mom. I just hate doing everything different."

I told him that we should be grateful for insulin, that he could have a long life. He said, "No, Mom. It's not fun. I would rather live a short, happy life than a long, sad one."

I asked him to pray with me. "Dear God. Thank you for insulin that Ty can live a long life..."

Ty put his little hand over my mouth, interrupting me, saying, "No, Mommy. You aren't doing it right. I'll do it."

He went on, "Dear Father God. I am Tyler, your friend. I don't mind the shots. I just want to be a normal little boy with normal diabetes. Thank you. I love you. Amen."

He was five years old.

Tearfully, I tucked him in. Afterward, I went to my computer and worked on a multilingual beta Internet browser. This was around 1995. The Internet was exploding.

Normal Diabetes

Five-year-old Ty startled me a few hours later by walking into the room. He said, "Mommy, God gave me the answer. It's on the Internet, but it's not in American. You have to type 'normal diabetes'."

Ty sat on my lap as I used the multilingual beta browser. I typed in "normal diabetes." We found Dr. Kinga Howorka, professor of medicine at the University of Vienna, Austria. She is the founder of Functional Insulin Treatment and Diabetes Rehabilitation and Group Education, an ISO 9000 quality–certified patient education program.

Ty said, "That's it, Mom. That's it! Call them, Mommy. Call them now!"

I replied, "Ty, honey. It's nine o'clock at night. It would be something like four o'clock in the morning in Vienna, Austria. They live in a country far away and speak German."

Relentless, Ty said, "No, Mom. They will answer. Just call them."

And so I did. Amazed that Dr. Howorka answered her phone, I asked in my broken German if she spoke English. She replied, "Yes, of course, I speak English! Who is that?"

I explained that my little boy was sitting on my lap. I told her he prayed to God to live a normal diabetes life. I asked her what she did. Her response was "I simply do that to the best of my ability. I teach people to listen to their bodies and match insulin to the way they want to live, to their metabolism, instead of matching their lives to the demands of insulin."

We talked for a long while. She also sent me a copy of her book, *Functional Insulin Treatment: Principles, Teaching Approach and Practice for Medical Providers*.

It took several days to arrive. The foreword to her book is by Dr. Viktor Frankl, a prominent Austrian psychologist who wrote *Man's Search for Meaning* after surviving Auschwitz concentration camp during World War II. Dr. Howorka was his student and physician. I was—and continue to be—impressed.

There was also a foreword by Dr. Jay Skyler, past president of the American Diabetes Association, prominent endocrinologist, and research scientist. He works in Florida. We spoke the following day. He encouraged me to go to Vienna, learn, and report back to him on our experience.

Allen, Ty, and I boarded a flight to Vienna a few months later. Alec stayed home with Gilly, our au pair from South Africa. She is the one who speculated that Ty was ill after joining our family less than a week.

Allen took Ty on tours of Vienna while I sat through intensive diabetes group education for patients, interpreted by a German-to-English translator who whispered key points in my ear over the next eleven days. Ty and Allen would stop by when lab tests or diabetes insulin exercises were required. Functional insulin treatment is abbreviated as FIT by Dr. Howorka's patients.

Dr. Howorka asks her patients what their goals are during rehabilitation and education. I tried to speak for Tyler, but Dr. Howorka said in her direct, but respectful, way, "Mom, please be quiet. I am talking to Tyler."

Tyler was perfunctory. "I want to eat the corner piece of a birthday cake with lots of icing, root beer, real root beer, all of it, a hot dog on a bun and still feel good. I want to run whenever I want for as long and hard as I want to. I don't want to feel tired so much or have blurry eyes.

I don't want to eat if I don't feel like it, especially if I'm sick. I don't want to wet my bed anymore. And I don't want to take shots or die."

Dr. Howorka said, "My god, Tyler. Almost all of this is possible. You can eat, or not eat, run and play or rest. But you must take insulin in a shot. You cannot eat insulin because it turns to poop like food and does nothing. If you are willing to take more shots, in the right place, at the right time, in the right amount, for the right reasons, you can have the freedom to live this life you want. But you are not immortal, and I am not God. Of course, you will die. We will all die. That is not the question. The question is how do you choose to live?"

Heaven knows, I love this woman! She told Tyler he could only have FIT if he could do his own injections. He was almost six; we had been helping him practice injecting on his own—always supervised. Back then, Ty was too young to be offered an insulin pump. I lobbied for small infusion needles with a pump manufacturer. These are available today.

Ty never gave in. He disliked the idea of being attached to a pump or any machine. On FIT, Ty would need to take a minimum of four to six shots every day, maybe more, depending on his lifestyle choices.

In Ty's slow, painstaking way, he prepared himself to inject. Kinga couldn't stand it. She interjected, "Please stop! If you are taking five to ten minutes for every shot, you will not have a life. If you take six shots, that means one hour of your playtime. Do you want that? Just do it quickly and say, 'Ha ha! Diabetes, you will not take my playtime away!'"

Ty smiled, plunged the needle in straight through his pant leg and laughed. "Ha ha! To *you*, diabetes!"

I *really* love this woman!

After this success, Kinga turned to me. "So tell me, Mommy, what are your wishes and goals?"

I remember telling her, "I do not want Tyler to die from cerebral edema because some stupid person does not understand diabetes."

Cerebral edema is swelling of the brain, causing brain death. It is a condition of diabetic ketoacidosis (DKA), a severe high blood sugar condition causing unconsciousness, generally brought on by severe illness, dehydration, or insufficient insulin. DKA is a rare, but treatable, condition that can be fatal if untreated.

Tyler's one and only event of diabetes ketoacidosis happened in Japan. His death certificate reads diabetes ketoacidosis as the cause of death.

There is evidence that Tyler asked for medical attention, and none was provided. A People to People leader on Tyler's trip to Japan denies that Tyler asked for medical help. According to Japanese hospital officials, Tyler's death could have been prevented had he received immediate medical attention.

Tonsil Ick to Me
(Tonsilectomy)

Among many other things, Kinga taught me how to calculate the amount of insulin for glucose infusions if Ty needed to be in a hospital. That came in very handy a few years later when Tyler had his tonsils removed.

Allen and I were with Ty as he underwent anesthesia for a tonsillectomy. Anesthesia is a troubling and unnatural sleep. I tested his blood and injected insulin to get his blood sugars to the target levels the medical staff wanted. The tonsillectomy was performed.

Ty was crying for me. The medical staff had handed him a Popsicle. He wanted his mom. The nurse found me refilling my coffee and asked me to come. Ty held his arms out to me and unfolded into a meltdown, sobbing.

I checked his blood sugars; they were right on target. The medical staff was very impressed that we could predict Ty's blood sugars because we paid close attention to his metabolism. They asked me for Dr. Howorka's book. I handed them my only signed copy .

At home, when Ty's throat was healed enough that he could speak to me, he explained that he had seen a very bright sun, shining on tall green cactuses with arms that were holding a hot iron and burning his throat. I believe they covered Ty's eyes during surgery.

Surprised and perplexed, I explained that he had seen the doctors and nurses in green scrub clothing with a surgery light above him, and yes, they did cauterize his tonsils to stop bleeding.

Years later, I heard stories about patients under anesthesia describe how they left their bodies and observed the room from above. One story was from a person who saw a quarter on top of a cabinet that no one could see from below. Sure enough, the quarter was there.

Blessings Are To Be Shared

Ty's life was transformed by FIT and Dr. Howorka. We learned how to match his insulin to his life and metabolism. Tyler fasted for more than twenty-four hours without having a severe low blood sugar. He did not have to force carbohydrates or sugars if he was sick. He feasted on pasta, Italian ice cream, and sodas without having severe high blood sugars. Yay!

Tyler could still have moderate blood sugar highs from excitement, illness, or growth hormones, but these were easily and accurately corrected. Ty could celebrate birthdays and holidays with his friends! He was able to realize the normal little-boy diabetes life he wanted to live.

A few weeks after rehabilitation back in Minnesota, Ty grew four inches, exchanged a gray pallor for rosy cheeks, and put on some healthy weight. From that day forward, Ty's HbA1c diabetes health checks would be described as excellent to extremely excellent, with no severe low blood sugars requiring third-party intervention, categorized as level 3 or level 4 glycemic events.

Life was good again. In the photo is Tyler, age six, a few weeks after functional insulin treatment, or FIT. His testimony, along with others, was in a local paper.

We returned home extremely happy. On the plane, Ty told us, "When God gives you a blessing, you have to share it." We were excited to share our revelations with Ty's pediatric diabetes support group, his pediatrician, and Dr. Jay Skyler.

At the support group, Ty told his little friends that his mommy and daddy would help them get FIT, too. They surrounded us with laughter, hugs, and very huge expectations.

Tyler Hill, 1st grade

Over the next five years, Allen and I co-founded and managed FIT USA Foundation. FIT USA conducted multiple patient education programs and medical provider education programs in Austria and the United States. We had the FIT curriculum translated into English with the help of a multilingual translator at Mayo Clinic. FIT USA provided course materials to numerous American practitioners. Dr. Skyler was a catalyst in bringing Dr. Howorka's Functional Insulin Treatment Diabetes Group Education and Rehabilitation to the United States via Florida.

By divine grace and hard work, we never had an overabundance of funding, but resources would somehow arrive at the right time in the right place to make the demonstration projects in Austria and America a reality. People living with diabetes earned freedom and knowledge to live without fear, to enjoy life.

With FIT, Tyler's blood sugar results went from sometimes scary to extremely excellent. He never experienced a severe low blood sugar or a severe high blood sugar requiring third-party intervention while living with us.

One time, we were frightened when we missed an injection of base insulin during a Colorado ski trip when Ty was young. Ty was unable to keep anything down, his blood sugars were climbing, and he was dehydrated. He apparently had mountain sickness. A quick trip to the clinic for rehydration and Ty was just fine, hitting the ski slopes the next day.

Ty spoke at numerous nationally recognized diabetes advocacy fund-raisers, before National Institutes of Health fellows, and served as a role model for many kids with diabetes. He shared the blessing he was given—his normal diabetes life. I call it his exceptional diabetes life.

In 2007, Coach Augeson, Ty's rugby coach, coordinated his Western Alliance Rugby Team, a.k.a. the Warriors, in a memorial rugby match at Tyler's high school. Ty's school and teammates collected school supplies to send to his other coach, Ashley Horobin, who was serving in Iraq. Coach Horobin read a tribute to Tyler and America's fallen heroes over the Internet that was broadcast on loud speakers.

"We remember them at the rising and the setting of the sun." The photo is of Coach Horobin in Iraq with Tyler's memorial T-shirt. The back of the shirt has the Walking-on-Sunshine logo from the first edition of this book cover imprinted on the back.

Tyler, age 10, diabetes advocate

Ty , MVP, scoring at rugby

Tyler's rugby coach, Ashley Horobin, Iraq, 2007

Until Japan

Tyler traveled to Japan in 2007 on a People to People Student Ambassadors trip shortly after his sixteenth birthday. He was thrilled with what he thought was a nomination to represent America. Born on the anniversary of D-day, the opportunity to visit Hiroshima was intoxicating for him. Ty died in Japan. His death devastated our family and our community.

Tyler was four years old when he told me Heaven called his name. Perhaps the Divine called Ty by his heavenly name a second time. This time, without me by the bedside to plead with the Divine and Tyler, Ty chose Paradise.

A few months after Tyler's funeral, the license plate for my car arrived. It felt like a message from Heaven: TL 461. T and L are the first and last initials of Ty's name. Sixty-one read sixteen to me—the last birthday Ty would celebrate with us. Ty had been four years old when Heaven called him by his real name.

Years prior, when Ty was diagnosed with diabetes at age five, I asked the diabetes center how many healthy years Ty could expect. They told me fifteen years.

Several years later, Tyler's wrongful death lawsuit settled shortly before trial after Judge Porter granted our motion to amend the complaint to add a claim for punitive damages.

Allan, Alec, and I were in Alaska, putting my mother's ashes in the earth next to my father's, when the CEO of the student travel company issued a press release on my birthday, June 22, 2009, with surreal timing:

> *Ambassador Programs, Inc. announced today, that on June 17, 2009, its parent company, Ambassadors Group, Inc. ("AGI"), and the plaintiffs settled all claims, matters and disputes pursuant to the lawsuit filed by Allen Hill and Sheryl Hill. The settlement agreement executed by all parties provides that the terms of the settlement are confidential. However, AGI believes that the terms of the settlement, whether viewed individually or in the aggregate, do not and will not have a material adverse effect on the Company.*
>
> *Jeff Thomas, president and chief executive officer of Ambassadors Group, Inc. and chief executive officer of Ambassador Programs, Inc. stated, "We are very pleased that our lawsuit with the Hill family has been resolved. Through hindsight we can see that there are steps that all of the leaders should have taken that could have prevented Tyler's death on June 29, 2007, during a trip to Tokyo Japan, and regret that they were not taken. We are very sorry for Tyler's death and the Hill Family's loss and the impact it has had on many. We continue to review all policies surrounding students with pre-existing conditions, including diabetes protocols, to refine our procedures. Ambassador Programs remains committed to developing and operating programs which promote and encourage world peace and global education through people-to-people exchange."*

Every Ending is a New Beginning

I was startled awake in a hotel room in Philadelphia at half past midnight. I was there with two ambitious twelve-year-old Minnesota preteens who dreamed of championship hockey. They were playing for USA Hockey on the CAN/AM team. My younger son, Alec, was one of the goalies. I was the team manager. One of Alec's best buddies was with us.

The two boys were sleeping on a pullout sofa in the next room. Alec got up, screaming and pacing. "Get the queue! Get the queue! The house is falling! The house is falling! Nnnnyyyyhhh! Nnnnyyyhhh! Mom! Get the queue! The house is falling! We have to go! TY! TY! TY! TY! TY!"

I grabbed him and pulled him to me, saying, "Shhhh! It's okay! You're having a night terror. Breathe, Buddy."

He didn't calm down, repeating the same message over and over, screaming, "The house is falling! The house is falling! Get the queues, Mom! We have to go! Nnnyyyyhhh! TY! TY! TY!"

His eyes looked like Tyler's once did, a deer's shining in the headlights, seldom blinking. He grabbed my hand and jerked me toward the door, screaming the same mantra over and over.

In exasperation, I grabbed him firmly and said, "Alec! You have to shut up! We are in a hotel! Someone is going to call the police! You sound like you are being hurt!"

Alec was crying and hyperventilating. His Buddy woke up. I told his friend that Alec was having a night terror and asked him to grab a nighttime pain reliever from the bathroom and a cup of water.

I asked Alec if he knew who I was.

He said, "God! Mom! Get the queues!"

By then, I realized he meant, "Get the keys!"

I said, "Buddy, we can't go anywhere. It's the middle of the night."

"Mom. We have to go! I love you. The house is falling! We have to go! Nnnnnnnyyyyyyyhhhhhh! Aaaaaggghh! Come! Now! TY! TY! TY!"

Caressing him more softly now, I took the pill from his friend and put it in Alec's mouth.

Placing the cup of water next to Alec's lips, I said, "Shh, baby. Shh! It's okay. I'm here. I love you. Everything is okay. You had a night terror. We are all fine. You need to take this and try to calm down and sleep. Come lie on my bed, and I'll rub your back."

He whimpered, but obliged me. His whimpering was relentless all night. His Buddy slept alone on the sofa. Alec slept next to me on the king-size bed.

Alec awoke the next day without memory of the night before. His teammate told him, "Dude, that was so weird."

We went on with the day's events, agreeing to take a young Czech girl for the night so her parents could tour New York. Her father was the coach of the Czech hockey team, so it seemed like the right thing to do. What is one more preteen, anyway?

Japan is more than a half day ahead of Philadelphia. At the approximate time that Alec was having a night terror fright about Tyler, Ty was dying half a world away.

The next morning, I was startled awake in Philadelphia by my cell phone. Allen, my husband of more than twenty years, called, distressed and concerned. With angst, he told me what he knew. Without reiterating minutiae, Ty's Japanese medical record reflected that his heart stopped for about one and a half hours before it was resuscitated. Ty was in grave condition. Grave is defined as preparation for a corpse. My heart felt like lead. Ty was leaving us.

The three tender, preteen hearts entrusted to my care were woken up by my wrenching grief and wailing. I called Allen back to say I was going to Japan. He said he was coming, too. All the while, the boys were scared, crying, and looking at me for help. I told the young Czech girl not to worry, and that I would not leave her until she was safely in the care of someone she knew.

I literally threw stuff into luggage and hockey bags while calling the ice arena. I explained, "My son is dying in Japan. I have to leave. I have to leave. NOW! Please send someone to the airport to pick her up!"

One hand on the wheel, the other on the phone, partially blinded by tears, I arrived at the airport. Tournament officials showed up shortly after us with grief-stricken faces and took the young Czech girl. She wrapped her arms around us and put small gifts in our hands, all the time saying, "Sorry. I am so sorry."

I honestly can't remember what happened to the car rental. I think I left it on the curb with the keys in the ignition and the agreement on the seat. My two boys had to pee, so I told them to stick together and come right back. I watched them take off to the bathroom.

I yanked the hockey bags out of the vehicle with a fury. No one dared help me. I was a wreck. Kicking, shoving, wailing, and crying, I dragged two hockey bags and three suitcases to the door.

Somewhere in the midst of the chaos, an incredible, heart-centered black woman working for the airline came up to me. She took the bags from me and said, "I don't know what's going on. I just know you need to be held." She wrapped those big, loving arms around me, and I collapsed onto her breasts, sobbing.

She took control. The boys found us at the counter. She escorted us through ticketing, security, up to the gate, then directly onto the plane to Minneapolis. She kissed my forehead and told me God was in control.

On the plane, Alec cocooned tearfully into a pillow against the window. His friend, anxious and upset, kept asking if Ty was going to be all right. I kept telling the boys, "We can hope and pray."

Across from me, a lovely young woman named Sue introduced herself. She told me she had recently been widowed. She had three beautiful young girls. Her friendship, perseverance, and faith gave me strength. One of her daughters, about the same age as Alec and his friend, comforted and distracted them for the duration of the trip home to Minneapolis.

Sue somehow remembered us and contacted us two and a half years later. She was at the right place for us at the right time.

Minneapolis, June 2007

A lec could not come with us to Japan. His passport had expired. In hindsight, I am thankful. Alec was spared the grueling reality of Ty's departure.

With heavy hearts, we handed Alec off to his very loving Aunt Candace, Allen's older sister. She and Alec were to go to Chicago to expedite getting passports and join us in Japan as soon as possible.

We sent Alec's friend through the security door to reconnect with his dad, who was right there waiting for us. We hugged and kissed Alec and his aunt, lingering as long as possible before the gate door was closed. In the back of my mind, I was saying good-bye to my younger son, while traveling to say good-bye to my older son.

En route to Japan, June 2007

T he airline was acutely aware of our trauma. We were placed in business class. I asked the stewardess if she could ask the pilot for a status on Ty at the Japanese Red Cross Hospital. A few hours later, she came with a teletype that said Ty was stable, but in grave condition. Nothing had changed.

I was hyperventilating. Allen was tearful. We clung to each other. Allen reached into my bag and gave me two of the same nighttime pain-relieving sleep-aid pills I had given Alec only one short day ago. He asked me to try and rest. We were in for a fourteen-hour flight.

I had a vision from Ty. He said, "Mom, I am sorry. I am not going to make it. I love you. Love Dad. Love Alec."

I screamed and wailed and jerked. Allen tried to hold me, saying, "Shhh! What's happening?"

I said, "Ty came to me. He told me he is not going to make it. He died, Allen. Oh, my God! Ty is dead."

Allen said, "Sheryl! Stop! You have to keep thinking and believing positive."

I said, "No, Allen. Look at your watch. I'm telling you. He died." Neither one of us could rest.

Tokyo, Japan, June 2007

I desperately wanted someone who loved and cared about Tyler to be close to him. Abbey, Tyler's girlfriend, told me later that she also wanted to be with him. She was at the hospital when we arrived, as she also participated in the student travel program to Japan.

Abbey was in the waiting room of the Japanese Red Cross Medical Center when we arrived. Ty's medical doctors explained to us that sometime during the night, Ty's brain began to swell. They tried to relieve the swelling by drilling into his skull to relieve pressure. They were unsuccessful.

Ty's body was being sustained by artificial respiration. His brain had died about the time I told Allen to look at his watch.

We asked if we could be with Ty. Abbey, Allen, and I went in with the staff. We talked to him and touched him to see if his heart rate or blood pressure would change—nothing.

I lifted Ty's eyelid, hoping for a spark of life. Those beautiful brown eyes were lifeless and dull. I kissed him on the cheek because his lips were obstructed by the respirator. I could not run my hands through his beautiful thick brown hair or kiss him on the forehead because his head was wrapped in a gauze turban. His body temperature was lowered as a precaution. Allen held Ty's cold, lifeless hand, kissed his fingers, and told Tyler how much he loved him.

The Japanese staff was extremely courteous, respectful, and helpful. They did everything within their power and within the law to help us take Ty's body home. They asked us about organ donations and told us to take our time.

We did not need to take time. It was Ty's decision. He had checked the box on his driver's license only weeks earlier.

At the Japanese Red Cross Hospital in Tokyo, we were informed that Ty could be taken off life support the next day. They advised us to go to the hotel and try and rest. Abbey came with us.

Abbey's name means "sanctuary." It was comforting to have her with us although, like us, she was having a hard time coping. The Japanese medical staff gave each of us a sedative to help us sleep. It didn't help. We ended up feeling drugged and unable to walk.

Chicago, June 2007

We phoned Chicago to reach Alec and his aunt Candy to tell them the solemn news about Tyler. She was alone with Alec at a hotel. They had ordered in and were waiting to hear about the passport.

Alec came to the phone. I said, "I'm so sorry, Buddy. Ty didn't make it." I heard him cry. His aunt picked up the phone and said she needed to comfort Alec.

Later, Alec would tell me that he knew before I phoned because Ty had come to him and said, "I'm not going to make it, Bro. Take care of Mom and Dad." Alec then wrote a poem, a tribute for his brother. He was twelve. His paternal uncle read it at Tyler's memorial.

A New Life
by Alec Hill, Tyler's brother

You have taught me well
You have made me strong.
I thought learning was hard
I guess I was wrong.
Laughter, memories
All of which you made.
I thought it was forever
Until it starts to fade.
Though I fear not
Going through strife
For you have started
Started a new life.

Tyler's D-day, June 2007

We had asked for an English-speaking minister to pray Ty's soul to Heaven and bless him. When we arrived at the Japanese hospital, the minister was already there. We were all tearfully somber. The minister prayed with us and over us.

Then we went into the emergency room chamber where Ty's body was artificially breathing behind a screened curtain. Japanese hospital staff were standing respectfully beside Tyler. The minister blessed Tyler, commending his soul to Heaven. We held Tyler, kissing him good-bye as the respirator made its scraping noise out of our son's airway.

Heavenly Distraction

By some act of grace, we thought it was over when the breathing tube had been removed from his mouth. Abbey, Allen, and I clung to Ty a while longer, until it became unbearable. Then we left the critical care room. We clenched each other in a furious, anguished hug in the hallway. I felt my skin pulling from me upward. Later, we would learn that Ty's heart stopped four minutes later.

Dr. Lerma wrote in his book *Learning from the Light* that the souls of dear ones we love do not want us there when they leave their body, 80 to 90 percent of the time. According to Dr. Lerma, angels create a thought or a distraction to pull us away so our dear ones will not be concerned about us and can depart in peace. Dying patients often see angels in the upper left corner of the room. I like believing that Ty was escorted by many angels into his new life.

Every Ending is a New Beginning

I have a friend who founded "1in100," an initiative to inform parents of newborns about a simple, inexpensive test to identify the one in one hundred babies born with heart defects. She confirms that the majority of the time, parents who hold vigil by their dying baby's side leave for a moment when their babies pass away.

Ty's death certificate reads that he died on June 29. While that may be technically true, I think he died before that. I believe that his soul was reaching out to us on the other side of the world when his heart was stopped on June 27, when Dr. Yagi worked heroically to resuscitate him.

Red Tape

There was much Japanese and United States red tape to bring a body home. The United States Embassy suggested that we cremate his body and bring the ashes home. But I knew. I knew that Ty wouldn't want that because that would be hot, like Hell. So we declined. His body could not come home with us the next day. Ty's body arrived a few days later, on July 3, 2007.

Proud American

Ty had always been a history buff. In kindergarten, he would play endless hours with little green army men, creating battle fields and strategies, sometimes with dinosaurs threatening.

He grew up reading books about Genghis Khan, Geronimo, World War I and II, and anything about D-day, especially history written by

Stephen Ambrose, such as *Band of Brothers*. Ty watched the History Channel for fun. He subscribed to *Military Magazine*. Ty was enrolled in Advanced Placement History for his upcoming junior year. His favorite holiday was the Fourth of July, American Independence Day.

We couldn't hold Ty's memorial service on July 4, so we waited until July 5. Friends and family who heard the news came by with condolences. I told Alec that there might not be many people at the service because Ty's body was in Japan until July 3, and the 4th was a holiday. We couldn't submit the obituary notice because newspapers aren't published on July 4.

Our family and friends comforted us as we all went out on the lake and watched fireworks explode in the night sky over the bay. Fourth of July celebrations were one of Ty's favorite things. We felt like Heaven was celebrating Ty's homecoming.

A Celebration of Life

On July 5, we went through the motions of preparation for our final good-bye to our boy and brother. My dear friend, Denise, had taken on the burden of preparing Tyler's memorial service while we were in Japan. Ty's service was incredibly beautiful, filled with promise, respect, and love. Over six hundred people attended. Many had to stand in the halls of the chapel. We had planned on two to three hundred for a luncheon. Text messaging, Facebook, and MySpace pages prevailed. I am so grateful to social media!

Denise read from the book, *The Next Place*, by Warren Hanson. *The Next Place* is a splendidly illustrated book describing the next place we go after this life. One verse speaks about the circle of our spirits shining brighter than the sun, explaining, "The love, friendship and happiness will travel with us, making our spirits glow, in the light that shines forever, in the next place that we go." *The Next Place* resonates for me as much as Ty's spirit book. More on Ty's spirit book later.

Wally, director of Huber Funeral Homes, phoned the hotel hosting the luncheon and told them to knock down some walls and triple up. I love Wally. He has interred three people that I love, including Tyler.

Denise's husband, Max, died four months after Tyler. He was blowing leaves off the roof and suffered a fatal fall. My mother died in hospice care at our home one and half years after Ty's death.

Death always seems to hit me in threes. Three loved ones died in three years: Dad, Sherry, and Joshie, then Ty, Max, and Mom.

Channeling

At the luncheon planned for Ty's memorial, the mother of one of the kids on the tour with Ty tried to approach me, but collapsed at my feet. I called out for a doctor and 911. I asked someone to get an aspirin. Wally was already in action. I thought the mom was having a heart attack. I later learned that she had one lung and had suffered an anxiety attack. A few weeks later, I would run into the mom and daughter again. The mother told me the paramedics put needles into her arm. A bruise had appeared on her arm that spelled "Ty."

Kids who were on Ty's trip to Japan came to his service wearing T-shirts with "R.I.P. Ty! Walking on Sunshine" written on them. They told me that Ty had wanted to run up Mt. Fuji because he wanted to get to the top to be closer to God. He was the first one up. Ty was singing *Walking on Sunshine* (written by Kimberley Rew for Katrina and the

Waves, 1983). I learned later that Mt. Fuji means "never ending" or to "never die." Mt. Fuji is a volcano that has been sacred since ancient times.

Ty's Sun Castle

The body that clothed Ty's soul was placed in a crypt in a new mausoleum less than twenty minutes from our home. His granite marker is inscribed with *Walking on Sunshine*. The mausoleum has two magnificent stained glass windows of an abstract sun at both ends. One stained glass sun window catches the eastern sun as it rises. A skylight shines down on a granite mosaic of an abstract sun on the floor when the sun is overhead, and one stained glass sun window catches sun rays as the sun sets in the west. The mausoleum is bright with sunshine.

We call it Ty's Sunshine Castle. Ty loves the sun! Christ is often symbolized as the eternal sun in scriptures. Every ending is a new beginning.

Tyler on Mt. Fuji, the day before
his heart stopped

Tyler's inscription

Ty's Sun Castle (mausoleum)

Four to Six Weeks

D r. Lerma, author of *Into the Light*, told me that in his experience helping thousands to depart from this life in palliative care, the soul somehow alerts its person that he or she is going to pass about four to six weeks before the body dies.

Dr. Lerma also talks in his books about how people near death want to be close to those most special to them before they die.

The night before Ty went to Japan, he and his little brother, Alec, kept sneaking into each other's rooms and talking. By about two o'clock in the morning, I was getting frustrated. I told the boys that Ty had to be up very soon, and they needed to go to sleep.

Alec told Ty he needed a happy memory so he wouldn't miss him too much. Ty did a bunch of crazy wrestling moves on the floor that cracked us up. We were all laughing. He and Alec did their bro handshake for the last time that early morning, ending with "Peace! Power! Love! Good luck, Bro!"

A Gift of Wisdom

Mother's Day was about a month before Ty's trip. Traditionally, my husband and my two boys surprised me by planting a Mother's Day love garden for me near a boulder at the end of our driveway. It's a small piece of earth, perhaps four feet by two feet in the shape of an arc.

My guys would wait until I was preoccupied or running an errand to plant their flowers. They usually planted a handmade cardboard sign filled with love messages for me next to the spot. We enjoy that garden and its meaning all season.

That year, Ty told me he decided to plant a perennial. He said he was going to plant a perennial every year until he went away to college. That way, I would always have love flowers from him in the Momsy Garden.

One day, while I was shopping for flowering additions to my yard, a master gardener told me, "Russian sage is symbolic for wisdom and knowledge. It grows well in the sun and has a lovely healing herbal scent."

Ty's Russian sage plant dominates its small space. Ty will never plant another love flower in my Mother's Day Momsy Garden. I am ever so thankful for his sage healing gift of wisdom and knowledge.

Eternal Sun

Ty loved the sun. He loved the sun because he learned that vitamin D is a great healer. Ty's favorite color was bright yellow. He wanted his room painted that color. We compromised and muted it to a golden yellow. Ty chose an abstract sun mural for the wall above his bed. He would sometimes say to me, "I'm going outside to catch some rays." Sun symbols became magnificently resplendent for us after Ty's death.

Foresight

Tyler signed our family up to host a foreign exchange student with Youth for Understanding one month before he died. That act would become a saving grace in future years.

Momsy Love

Two or three days before Ty left for Japan, he told me that he wanted to spend all day with me doing whatever I wanted. I explained that we left too many things undone. I would be running errands. He wanted to come along and invited his girlfriend, Abbey.

We had such a fun day! We shopped for clothing and had lunch. Ty wanted a book to read on the long flight, and found a book on Genghis Khan that appealed to him.

He also came to me with a book extremely out of character for him. The book had six hundred plus pages of information about spirits, evidence of life after death, and some spooky stuff. It cost about $25 and weighed several pounds. Spooky stuff freaked Tyler out. Movies like *Signs* and *The Sixth Sense* made it hard for Tyler to fall asleep.

I told Ty I didn't think that book was a good idea. It was big and bulky and filled with ghosts and dead people and was pretty expensive. He must have put that book back on the shelf half a dozen times.

As I was checking out, he came up to me with the book and said, "Mom, I'll buy it with my money." I bought the book *Real Ghosts, Restless Spirits, and Haunted Places* by Brad Steiger.

Ty never took the book with him to Japan. I found it lying on his bed when we returned, grief stricken after he died. I remember feeling annoyed at how he insisted on getting that book and relieved that he took my advice. I am ever so grateful that he bought it. I call this book Ty's spirit book.

Old Man Love

That the same day, Ty asked me to help him pick out free weights and a bench for his dad's fiftieth birthday, which was coming up in July.

He said, "Dad and I are going to get ripped this summer." He was so satisfied with his purchase. Tyler paid money down with funds he earned from a neighborhood job mowing lawns. Ty liked to refer to his dad as his "Old Man," even before Allen was fifty.

A few days prior, Tyler had spent time with me planning a surprise dinner cruise for his dad's fiftieth birthday with about thirty-five family members and close friends. He also picked out a birthday card for his dad that read, "I love you mower and mower."

Ty's death was one month before his dad would celebrate his fiftieth birthday. We decided to honor Ty and Allen by continuing with the dinner cruise party that Ty helped plan.

The dinner cruise tripled in guests. So many friends, family, and neighbors wanted to show love and support for Allen. The largest boat we could rent was at capacity. Boats followed behind us wearing *Walking on Sunshine* shirts. There was not a cloud anywhere in the blue sky. It was a vibrant hot day.

Ooh Aah

Ty created a MySpace page so that he could share his experiences in Japan with friends without having to write multiple e-mails. The song he chose as background music was *Ooh Aah* by Grits, a Christian band. *Ooh Aah's* lyrics are as follows:

I'm on an island by my lonesome stranded
Low key and stayin' candid
Reflectin' on the things I try my hand at
Search for the equations to persuasions I'm used to
Findin' comfort in the zones of closet bones I get loose to
A mountainous fontaine,
Spinnin' and monsoonin'
Grinnin' its high octane
This worlds out wacky
Rollin' down the hills cause life's a hassle
Encircled by my folly like a moat surround a castle
Stay afloat,
Catch a second wind thin is the air I breathe
Teary-eyed nose runnin', wipe the snot on my sleeve
I'm callin' on my savior to be all that I need
Please forgive me my behavior had me lost at light speed

The song resonates with me. The *island stranded* is Ty alone in his hotel room halfway around the world on an island, Japan. A *mountainous fontaine* speaks to me of Mt. Fuji's spiritual pull, enticing Ty to run, not walk, to the highest point to be closer to God, to never die.

Teary eyed because he was sick, needing medical attention, realizing his fate, knowing his powerlessness, relying on higher power.

Thin is the air I breathe. Dehydration causes blood to become very viscous. Oxygen has a hard time reaching cells. Organs slowly suffocate until failure and death.

I've heard grieving parents say that the world kept turning the same way after their child died. I did not feel that. An earthquake shook Japan shortly after Ty's death. It was threatened by a hurricane (*spinnin' and monsoonin'*). Torrential rains caused flooding in Minnesota. People were dying and losing their homes. The I-35W Mississippi River Bridge in the Twin Cities collapsed.

I cried out to Heaven, "Enough. Please stop. Please make it stop."

Please forgive me my behavior had me caught at light speed.

Ty wrote in his journal of the Tokyo bullet train, "I feel like my life is fast forwarding in front of me."

Encircled by my folly like a moat surrounds a castle—Stay afloat.

Ty also wrote in his journal, "After Nijo Castle, we visited the Golden Pavilion, which was very intriguing. It was fantastic to be walking through the gardens and turn a corner to be utterly surprised by a castle completely covered by gold leaf. It was like seeing a glimpse of Heaven on earth that took my breath away and made me speechless."

In *Into the Light,* Dr. Lerma describes how patients review their life. Their progression into the light is based on their love and forgiveness of their conscious actions. I know Ty was trying to stay afloat to say good-bye to us. It's uncannily bizarre to experience messages from him like we do.

Ty used to tell me that he never wanted to be called a Christian, although he believed in Jesus. He explained to me that too much devastation had happened in the name of Christ such as religious wars and inquisitions. The world didn't get all rosy because Christ came to earth; quite the opposite. Ty didn't like believing in an angry and jealous God who enslaved and destroyed his people. Tyler believed his Heavenly Father is all about love. One of Ty's all-time popular sayings was "Give me some love!" Ty believed that our souls evolve similar to reincarnation, but in Paradise, based on how much we love.

I'm callin' on my savior to be all that I need
Please forgive me my behavior had me lost at light speed.

I believe with my whole heart that Ty is in glory and love, in the light of the world, eternal sun—light speed, anywhere and everywhere at once, energy (NRG) all over the universe, conscious oneness.

Abbey Goddess

The month before Ty and Abbey went to Japan, they would cruise neighborhoods and speculate about their dream home. They mapped out that they would have four kids and named each one. They were hilarious in their role playing, very fun and animated. In Japan, they had a mock wedding and reception at a castle shortly before Ty became mortally ill.

Abbey and Ty went to prom a few weeks before Japan. They had a remarkable time. Ty gave Abbey—his "Abbey Goddess"—an amethyst pendant necklace. Amethyst is known as the bishop's stone. It is still worn by Catholic clergy and symbolizes spiritual wisdom, like my Mother's Day sage plant. Apparently, worn as a necklace, amethyst focuses energy. It is used as an aid in meditation.

Love Eye in Heaven

For prom night, Abbey bought Ty a boutonniere with a shimmering peacock feather decorating it. I later found it pinned to Ty's window shade. At his funeral, Abbey put a similar boutonniere on Ty's lapel, also with a beautiful peacock feather on it. I asked her what the feather meant. She said she didn't know.

I did some research on peacock feathers some time later. Peacock feathers are solar symbols. The sun is symbolic for us, knowing Ty is with us in the light of the world. Peacock feathers are an emblem of resurrection, immortality, incorruptible soul, paradise, and beauty.

Who could guess? I read that peacock feathers resemble the process of glorification, exchanging the earthly body for one in Paradise. So be it! Peacock feathers signify all-seeing wisdom from Heaven. My favorite interpretation is a love eye in Heaven.

Messenger from God

Abbey also placed a small felt deer in Ty's hand at the funeral. She had bought it when they toured a famous shrine called Miyajima. Deer are everywhere at Miyajima. Abbey took a tender photo of Ty kneeling, holding his hand out to a deer who is nuzzling his fingers. These deer are symbolic for messengers of God.

Abbey's photo of Tyler and a small deer at
Miyajima Shrine, Japan

Donor

Tyler passed his driver's license exam on his sixteenth birthday, June 6, about two weeks before he left for Japan. He came home, oh so proud, and showed me the yellow certificate that gave him a newfound freedom.

He said, "Mom, I checked the box to be an organ donor. Did you?"
I said, "Yep."

"Does that freak you out? I mean that somebody else will be using your body parts?" Ty asked.

"I don't think I'll care. I'll be dead."

He went on, "What do you want them to do with the leftovers?"

"I don't know. Bury me."

"No way, Mom. Six feet under with worms and bugs. Yuck."

"What then, cremation?"

"No, Mom. Hot like Hell."

"Well, Ty, what then?"

"I don't know, but I'm only sixteen. It feels good to know someone else's life could be better because I was here."

And then he asked me, "Mom, do you think God has something big planned for your life?"

"Yes, Bud, I do. You and Alec are my something big."

"No, Mom, I think God has something really big planned for you, besides me and Alec. What do you think it is?"

"I don't know, Bud. What about you?" I asked, smiling.

Smiling back, he said, "I don't know, Mom, but I think I'm going to find it in Japan."

Eternal Love

Ty and Abbey went to a Japanese school with Tyler's Japanese host mother. There they learned how to script in Japanese kanji. There is a photo of Tyler holding up his rendition of "eternal love."

Ty scripted *Eternal Love* in Japanese

Three Wishes

While going through his school backpack a few weeks after his death, I found Ty's tenth-grade health homework :

My Three Wishes

1. I wish for world peace, that people would stop hurting each other.
2. I wish that my family would never worry for money.
3. I wish that I would not die by someone else's mistake.

There was another page behind it. Ty's handwriting had left indentations in the paper. I held the paper up to the light and could make out the heading: *You Can't Escape Fate.*

Mountainous Fontaine

Ty had a tremendous respect for our neighbor. Ty didn't start playing hockey until he was thirteen. Not cool in cold, wintery Minnesota. Our neighbor was the Hockey Association president. He lobbied to help Ty join a team when Ty missed registration. Ty had a way of remembering acts of kindness.

So when Ty needed a written reference to go to Japan, our neighbor was the first person he went to. It isn't hard to imagine what our neighbor must have felt when he learned Ty died on the trip for which the neighbor had provided a recommendation.

We received a heartfelt letter from the neighbor. He was away in Colorado and could not attend Ty's funeral. He took a lone walk into the mountains, stacking smooth stones one on top of another, creating a cairn, hoping passersby might stop and reflect on this spot.

I will paraphrase his letter because I treasure his intent; it's personal. His message was one comparing Ty to the Colorado Rocky Mountains—majestic yet humble, strong yet fragile. He felt Ty's presence in the whisper of a breeze and the sun upon his face. He sent love up to our beloved son in a glorious way. A cairn marker tells the tale.

How can one know whose lives you impact? Whose hearts you touch? The hockey team Ty played for had a roast when he moved up to the next level. The captain gave him flowers because he was a "beast with a heart." Ty had scored two goals his first game and earned a reputation for a hockey defenseman who "checked" on the opponent when they went down after he "checked" them.

We received a treasured gift from the same neighbor and his daughter shortly after the third anniversary of Ty's memorial. They had hiked up the mountain to the place of honor and memory. Overnight, sunny yellow coreopsis had bloomed everywhere in the rocks and fields. Coreopsis flowers are symbolic for always being cheery.

Our neighbor dropped off enlargements of the sunny flowers. There was also a photograph of his daughter holding a memorial *Walking on Sunshine* bandana that Ty's school had handed out with T-shirts at a tree-planting memorial near the football field.

She told me that she carries this bandana with her everywhere. She takes photos with it when she is inspired by serenity, wonder, or awe of

Kacie and Erin with a "Walking on Sunshine" bandana

the beauty of the earth, magnificence. She has an album full of Ty's bandana moments. Feel the love.

The morning after I received their photos of sunshine-yellow coreopsis in the mountains on the anniversary of Ty's memorial, I took my coffee on the dock. The lake looked like mirrored glass, barely a ripple. I wanted to sit on the dock, reflect, and be thankful for friends, neighbors, the people we have in our lives, and the time we have with them, and love. I was waiting in anticipation for my morning view of the sunrise and its reflection on the water. What a sunrise! I took a photo with my phone to capture the moment. The photo rewarded me with a *sun* flower.

The sun flower at sunrise

Dragonflies and Indigo

About a week before Ty turned sixteen, I hired a handyman, Mark, to come to my house and paint the garage. Mark has traveled all over the world, studying and experiencing religion. I needed to reorganize the garage because Allen and I surprised Tyler with a used Kia a couple of weeks before his sixteenth birthday. Ty had maintained honor roll status. The car was his reward and motivation to keep his grades high and become more independent.

Mark asked me to run to the hardware store for paint. I found a very cool dragonfly stamp and metallic-green paint while I was waiting for Mark's paint to be mixed.

Ty and I often had dragonflies land on us when we were outside. We could pass them back and forth. It was fun. I thought I would stamp some metallic-green dragonflies up in the garage. Ty told me that my rendition of the dragonflies in the garage was awesome. They are still there—fond memories.

Ty came laughing into the garage with his girlfriend, Abbey, shortly after I finished. Mark commented to Tyler, "What a beautiful young man. You are graced by Heaven. You have an indigo aura around you. God has a great purpose for you. You must be an indigo child."

Mark had just met Ty, but he came back later with a balloon and an Eisenhower silver dollar for Tyler's birthday. I do not know how Mark knew that Ty admired President General Eisenhower or that Ty was leaving on a trip to Japan. I found the silver dollar in Ty's clothing from Japan. I keep it in a safe place, reminding me to focus on peace, glorious peace.

Mark told Ty and Abbey that indigo children are spiritually connected to the divine with higher Christ consciousness. Ty told me he felt great because no one had ever told him that.

I told Ty that Mark was just a handyman, to which Ty replied, "And Jesus was just a carpenter."

Direct Source

About two months after Ty died, some of his friends were at my house. I wanted to know more about Mt. Fuji. We Googled it and learned that Mt. Fuji means to never die, to have everlasting life. I also learned from a Mt. Fuji Internet site that just days prior to Tyler's death, a tour of Middle Eastern indigo children took a spiritual hike up Mt. Fuji to be closer to God. Ty must have felt that energy, to be closer to God. Perhaps this is why he ran ahead.

Someone gifted me a copy of P. M. H. Atwater's book, *Beyond the Indigo Children*. Atwater explains how the new children have a deep, connected plane with the direct source—eternal love—the Divine, Spirit, Consciousness. She describes the new children as the next jump in the human race.

Dragonflies and Indigo

Walking on Sunshine

Kids at Ty's funeral wore T-shirts with *Walking on Sunshine R.I.P* written on them. Ty sang the song on his way up Mt. Fuji. Ty loved the sun, songs about the sun, and imagery of the sun.

Walking on Sunshine
Katrina and the Waves, recorded 1985 (used with permission)

I feel the love,
I feel the love,
I feel the love that's really real,
I'm walking on sunshine, ohh! oh!"

Transformation

Shortly after Ty's funeral, a friend gave us a book called *The Dragonfly Door,* by John Adams. The author lives less than eight minutes from our home. The story is about dying and transformation. Two water nymphs become very close friends in a marsh. One is transformed into a beautiful dragonfly when it left its life in the marsh. The other waits expectantly.

The same day, a neighbor brought me an invitation to a grief-counseling session with Anne Brooker, who founded the Dragonfly Project when she was just eleven years old. The Dragonfly Project sends out key chains with dragonflies on them to bereaved families of deceased children.

We received one shortly after Ty's funeral with a version of a story of the dragonfly written by Walter Cavert. Several other key chains followed.

Cavert's story describes young larvae living in the bottom of a pond who cannot understand why friends climb up a lily pad stem and then disappear. One larva had an overwhelming need to climb, so he told his friends he would come back and tell. Once transformed into a beautiful dragonfly with iridescent wings reflecting sunlight, he tried to attract their attention, but they did not recognize their friend. The moral of the story is, "Just because we cannot see or speak with our loved ones transformed by what we call death, does not mean they do not exist."

There was a glass jar with a red top that reminded me of a bug jar in Tyler's suitcase when I unpacked it. I kept it because it was Tyler's.

My next door neighbor and longtime friend, Barb, was creating a display of Tyler's favorite things to celebrate his life: hockey, *Band of Brothers*, *Warhammer*, football, rugby, music, scuba diving, friends, and family. She brought me the most perfect, huge black-and-silver dragonfly shortly after the key chain arrived.

The dragonfly had landed between our houses and died near her feet. She picked it up and brought it to me and said, "This is from Ty! Isn't it beautiful?" She did not know anything about the dragonfly key chain, story, or Anne Booker's project.

I looked at her. We both had tears and goose bumps. I told her about Anne Booker and the dragonfly story. Together, we took the dragonfly and put it in Ty's jar. I still cherish it.

The last note from me that Ty read in Japan was on a dragonfly note card. My words to him were, "Spread your wings and fly! I am so proud of you."

Honoring Ty's Life

Allen, Alec, and I went back to Japan on the anniversary of Tyler's seventeenth birthday. We wanted to follow his footsteps, meet the Japan that he said "Rocks!" and replace horrid memories with happier ones.

We visited Ty's host family for several days. His host mom, Shigemi, asked me what I would most like to do on Tyler's birthday. Her birthday was the day after Tyler's. I said I would most like to see Mt. Fuji. She replied that this was not possible because June is Japan's rainy season. I reminded her that Ty hiked Mt. Fuji in June on a warm day. She said it would be very rare. Suddenly, her husband called out. The news just announced that Mt. Fuji made a surprise showing. We hustled up to the roof to see clouds parting and Mt. Fuji in its full splendor. Mt. Fuji remained breathtakingly beautiful and visible for the entire day.

On our drive up to the station where we would begin our hike, Allen and I became tearful and sad. We were holding each other and trying to pull it together when Shigemi said, "Sher. Allen. Look up." There, in front of us, was a Japanese tour bus with *Be Joyful* written in English on the back.

Walking on Sunshine

Sunshine Dragonfly

On our last day in Japan, a sunshine-yellow dragonfly kept landing on Alec. We tried to shoo it away so we could go inside the building, but it was persistent. We took this photo when it landed on the door handle just before we entered. Remembering Anne Booker's dragonfly story, we felt Ty's presence.

Sunshine-yellow dragonfly in Japan, reminding us of Tyler

Sheryl Hill

The Spirit Book

Energy

Remember, Allen and I had to return to Minnesota without Tyler's body. Tyler's body came home a few days later, after the international procedures were in order, on July 3.

We were met at the airport by Alec and many relatives. Exhausted, sleep deprived, and inconsolable, we made what seemed to be the longest drive to our home.

My adult nieces and nephew, Christina, Amber, and Matt, whose mother and brother had died almost seventeen years before, had left their lives to console Alec while we were in Japan. They knew what it was like to have their brother and mother die tragically. Alec knew that they knew. There was an understanding camaraderie between them that can only be felt. They were and are a great comfort to him and us.

Once at home, Alec took my hand and asked me to come into Ty's room. Brokenhearted, I told him, "I need more time. I'm not ready."

Persistent, he followed me into my bedroom, grabbed my hand and tugged. "C'mon, Mom. Come with me. It's peaceful there. Trust me."

I took a shuddering breath and followed him.

There on the bed was the *Real Ghosts* book by Steiger that Tyler just had to have, his "spirit book." Ty did not take the book to Japan after all. I remember having mixed emotions—miffed that we spent all that money, and Ty not taking the book after all, and at the same time, relieved that Tyler followed my advice.

I smelled Ty's smell when we walked in: his chick-magnet cologne, musky male scent, and eucalyptus lotion.

Alec and I put our heads down on Tyler's pillow and held each other tearfully. Allen came in to join us. Somehow, Ty's spirit book fell onto the floor.

I looked down at it. Words jumped off the page, explaining that every living being has a bioelectric cycle that resonates at sixty hertz. The book explained, "Energy can neither be created nor destroyed, only transformed." I reached down, picked up the book, and put it on the nightstand.

The three of us took a brief but very restful nap, entwined in hugs on Ty's bed. It felt like Tyler's piece of Heaven on earth. We were

startled back to reality when other family and friends arrived, ringing the doorbell.

The Spirit Book

Merkabah

I stood up. The book fell onto the floor again. No one was near. This time, it opened to a photo of an interdimensional soul vehicle, described in the Old Testament as Merkabah. "The Merkabah," writes Steiger, "is the Divine Throne Chariot described in Ezekiel's mystical experience and is associated with Heavenly realms."

I later learned the meaning of Merkabah: *Mer* means light, *Ka* means spirit, *Bah* means body—light spirit body surrounded by counter rotating spirals of light energy, wheels within wheels, the soul chariot of ascension as described in Ezekiel as whirling wheels with spirits of living beings within them guarded by seraphim. I understand seraphim are the highest, most powerful beings in Heaven.

These soul vehicles are also known to the Egyptians as sun boats. Today, many call them soul, angel or spirit orbs, spheres, or chariots.

Christ Chariot of Spirit

In the Gnostic Society Nag Hammadi Library, I read the Apocrypha of James, translated by Francis E. Williams. The disciple James wrote that Christ appeared to him five hundred and fifty days after he had risen from the dead. James writes that Christ said, "I shall depart from you, for a chariot of spirit has borne me aloft . . ."

Apparently, these sun chariots of the soul can be sensed or heard; people can see them. Steiger writes that the famous solo astronaut, Lieutenant John Glenn, told *LIFE* magazine about seeing literally thousands of them glowing like greenish-yellow fireflies.

I recall thinking, "Yeah, right. If that were true I would have seen them before. After all, my dad, my sister-in-law, my nephew have died." I picked the spirit book up, carried it to my office, and filed it on a bookshelf.

Energy

A lec's bedroom door was open. His schoolbooks were on the floor. I went to pick them up and put them away. In his notebook were similar words, "You can't create or destroy energy. Energy can only be altered." I asked Alec about it. He shrugged and said, "We were studying that in science."

I felt like Heaven was sending me a direct message, twice.

Months later, I would pick Ty's spirit book up again and again to compare it to many Merkabah, soul-spirit chariot orbs, making brilliant appearances in our lives in high moments of love and remembrance.

Becoming One

Faith like a Child

As a toddler, Alec's eyes would dart about the room as if he were talking to someone. Gilly and I thought he must be seeing angels. He described two imaginary friends, whom he called *Reflection* and *Mirror*. He would talk and play happily with Reflection and Mirror. If we came into the room and asked who he was talking to, he would say, "My friends, but they left when you came in."

Imaginary Friends

We talked about imaginary friends with Alec's Early Family Childhood Education leaders and moms and also with his pediatrician. I was told that it was really common for toddlers and children to have special make-believe playmates.

There is also a correlation between creativity and intelligence in children who have imaginary friends. I hadn't thought about Mirror and Reflection for years.

P. M. H. Atwater made references in *The Big Book of Near-Death Experiences* about children who can see beyond normal viewing and remember being in their mother's womb. As a child, Alec shared some memories he had of not being able to move in my tummy.

Faith like a child—I often wonder if that means the innocence to see into the next realm with total trust and love.

Double Portion of Spirit

A lec told me that he had felt Tyler enter his body when Tyler died. I asked him, "How?"

"It's hard to explain," he said. "I can feel him. It's like we are together."

Alec's words reminded me of Elisha in Old Testament scriptures. Elisha asked Elijah for a double portion of his spirit. In the New Testament, John the Baptist has the power and spirit of Elijah. Why isn't it possible that Heaven, knowing Ty's love for his beloved brother, would gift Alec with a double portion of Tyler's spirit? What an awesome parting gift!

Love Bonds

A very dear book to me is *Bridge Over the River* (circa early 1900s). It is the story of a young soldier's spirit channeling to his sister. He describes how their spirits are closely aligned, and because of this divine connection, he can reach her. The brother talks about the magnificence of Heaven and Christ as resplendent as the sun. It is a magnificent healing book for grieving persons.

One of the questions the book addresses for me is what happens to people we didn't really like or respect on earth. Men like Hitler.

After death communication from Sigwart, "No separation exists for those who are connected by bonds of love, which never ceases, not through life, not through death!" I interpret that as meaning that where there is no bond of love, there is no connection, but rather, there is separation. I believe love creates a more glorious Heaven.

Full of Crap

Alec was lethargic and docile for weeks following Tyler's death. We tried numerous grief counselors. Alec would not participate. He became a limp noodle in the therapists' offices. He once told me the therapists were full of crap. I asked him why.

He said, "Mom, they tell me it is okay to cry. My brother just died, and they tell me it is okay to cry."

I stopped forcing the issue. Alec spent his time with friends and his cousins, who knew what it was like to have a sibling die. Alec expresses himself and honors Ty in his writing, art, and behavior. I learn from him.

Secret Fort and Handshake

A lec and Tyler had built a fort on a tree branch that hung out over the lake. They hammered some planks into an overhanging branch for roosting and spying at passing boats through tree leaves. You had to scale down an embankment in a poison ivy–infested woods to get to their fort. Only they knew the secret way to avoid the poison. The fort had been there for years. Their fort was particularly fun in deep snow and was a favorite getaway place. They must have created their secret bro handshake there, spending endless hours telling secrets.

One day, Alec went outside with a hammer. I heard the crack of the hammer's lonely echo. Alec was gone for hours. I was worried. He came sorrowfully into the house. His puffy eyes told a sad story of his grief.

He said, "It's done. I destroyed the fort. No one is ever going to go there again. I kicked the last board into the water and told Ty I love him and good-bye, Bro."

Bible Swear

T hen Alec did something startling. He went over to the bookshelf and grabbed a Bible. He brought it over to Allen and me and told us to put our hands on it because we were going to swear to God. We did as he asked. He was so desperate.

He said the words, and we repeated them. "I swear we will always be a family. That we will never divorce! I swear we will always be together for eternity!"

Becoming One

Marriage Camp

When Ty was in kindergarten, shortly after being diagnosed with diabetes, he came home and told us that he never wanted to be divorced. Ty must have misread our anxiety over his diabetes as a failure in our relationship. He said he always wanted us to be a family. He asked us why we didn't love each other. We told him of course we loved each other. He said he didn't believe that because if we loved each other, he would see it.

He told us that some kids in his class were getting divorced, and they didn't get to live with their mommies and daddies anymore. We told him we understood but that we loved each other and he should not worry.

That wasn't good enough. Ty came home the next day with the phone number of a classmate whose parents went to marriage camp. We couldn't read his kindergarten numbers; they looked like chicken scratches. I wrote a note to the classmate's mom asking her to phone me.

She told me that she and her husband were having some problems, but they went to Marriage Encounter, and it transformed their relationship. Ty eavesdropped as I was talking to her.

That night at dinner, Ty said Allen and I needed to go to marriage camp. We agreed because he seemed to need it so much. Gilly, our au pair, lived with us and was very familiar with Ty's insulin regimen and then-baby brother Alec absolutely adored her. Allen and I were looking forward to a weekend away with just the two of us. Little did we know!

The weekend turned out to be a communication session where we talked about things most couples just don't talk about. Allen and I cried, we laughed, we danced, we hugged, we kissed. We talked and talked and talked. We learned how to date again. We learned to have a date night every week to keep our love alive and ignited! It was an awesome, albeit emotional, weekend.

Ty ran out to meet us when we came home with the brightest, most loving eyes and expectation you can imagine in a five-year-old. He said, "How did it go?"

Allen and I grabbed Ty, kissing him and each other in a family hug. We told him it was the best marriage camp ever. We told him that we learned how to love each other and that we needed a date night every weekend. Ty never let us ignore that. Ever. As he grew, he would engage Alec so that Allen and I could reconnect for date night every weekend.

Alec carried Ty's marriage-camp flag when he made us promise to God that we would always be together, one family. A double portion of "soul."

Always a Family

Three years after Ty's angel day, we held a family baptism to celebrate Tyler's nineteenth birthday. We were immersed in Jenning's Bay in front of our house. Many friends came to share in our dedication.

Allen, Alec, and I repeated to each other and our friends and family: "You are my _____ [*son, wife, husband, mother, father, brother*]. I belong to you, and you belong to me. We belong to the Lord for all eternity."

We echoed the same words for Tyler: "You are our brother and son. You belong to us, and we belong to you. Together we belong to the Father, Son, and Holy Spirit for all eternity."

It had been very rainy for weeks prior, and my friends and neighbors worried about cancelling if it did not stop. I told them we were going to get wet anyway. I remember saying that I did not know what the weather was going to be in the rest of Minnesota, but at eleven o'clock on June 6, the sun was going to shine on us. And so it did, for about two hours before the thunder boomers rolled in and the downpour began again.

Angelic Anniversary

Broken Heart

Ty was interred in July, 2007. In August, I spent a night in the emergency room. I have aortic valve prolapse and mitral valve stenosis, apparently from rheumatic fever as a young girl. If I get upset, in times of stress or panic, my heart is not efficient. I hyperventilate, trying to push blood out of my lungs and replace it with air. If I am successful, I can calm down; if not, I can faint.

This night, I fainted. I woke up thinking, "Oh, thank God! It was a dream!" only to discover it was real: hyperventilate, faint, and spiral over and over. I called out to my husband that I needed help.

After that episode and Alec's choice of unusual diction for the Bible swear, Allen and I decided to go to grief counseling with a Christian ministry. We chose Wayzata Free Church (WFC). WFC has a female and a male minister who help with couples in counseling.

Allen and I each took a personality profile. We learned that Allen, like many men, does not like to talk about painful memories so that he can remain strong for his family and because it hurts to go there. Adversely, I, like most women, prefer to talk about painful memories to release the pain.

Angelic Anniversary

Date Night

Allen and I began counseling and were advised once again that we should date for our anniversary, reconnecting with that person, ourselves, and our spouse who captured our hearts for marriage.

It was tough. Allen and Alec gave me a necklace and earrings with Alec's birthstone in them. Ty was not part of the celebration.

We tried eating out, but our tears streamed during dinner. Our hopes and dreams for Ty to graduate, marry, and have children were gone.

Allen said he wished that he would have told Tyler how proud he was of him.

I told Allen Tyler knew that. I also said that I was so happy I had told Ty how much I loved him at the airport as Ty twirled me around, reaffirming that he was a mama's boy.

The pain was so intense over dinner that we left our dinners half finished.

We chose to take a drive in the country. A storm loomed on the horizon. We could hear thunder and see lightning, but decided to park on a dirt road by an apple orchard. We got out and stretched out across the hood, holding each other's hands, wondering what messages Heaven might send us.

Tears flowed down our faces as we watched a glorious harvest moon in August. It was so close we could see craters. As we watched, clouds blew in and crossed in front of the moon. They were captivating, with silver linings.

Angelic Healing

Soon, a cloud appeared in the shape of an angel. The angel cloud had a side view with a line angled across its head similar to a halo, and palms forming praying hands. It was a calming sight.

Immediately after the angel cloud passed, another angel cloud appeared, larger and even more glorious. The cloud shape had a similar halo line across the forehead. It had wings and a long robe. There was a hole where its heart would be. Allen and I each noticed it and commented, "Oh, wow!"

As the second angel cloud blew across the brilliant harvest moon, moon beams danced around it, filling the hole in the cloud angel's heart with light. That light was shining directly down upon us! It was miraculous. In the distance, we could hear thunder. Elijah—the Lord is my God.

We went home, happy we had shared this experience, snuggled into bed, and relaxed into sleep. We were sound asleep when Alec came into our room with the same *nnngh* sounds and trancelike eyes he had the night before we learned Ty was dying.

Channeling

We woke up startled. I said, "Alec, are you having a nightmare?"
He said, "Mom! Do you know who I am? I love you, Mom! I will always love you! Dad! I am proud of you, too! I am so very proud of you!"

I said, "Yes, baby! I know who you are! Thank you for loving me. Thank you for telling dad you are proud of him, too! We will always love you."

That was not sufficient. It was Alec's voice, but Tyler's words were being spoken. "Mom, did you hear me? I love you so much! Dad, I am so proud of you, too!"

I wrapped my arms around Alec and pulled him into bed with Allen and me. We were tearing up. We each held him, saying, "We love you, Alec. We love you, Tyler. We will always be a family. Shhh, be still. Let's rest."

Alec's breathing softened, and he slumbered.

I said, "Allen, that's so weird. It's like Ty came to us through Alec to confirm what we needed to hear the most, that Ty knew how much we loved him and that we are so very proud of him."

It was unreal how Alec said exactly what Allen had needed to hear at our tearful dinner, a double portion of Tyler's spirit.

Alec had no memory of what transpired when he woke up. His first words were, "What am I doing in here?"

The Purplest

There are many photos of Ty around the house. I need to see his face in every room. I also had Angela L., an artist friend, paint *Live Your Best Life* on a beam in my kitchen so that I could get through preparing dinners with less anguish.

Ty used to sit at the high bar and free sample my cooking with uninvited funny critiques while he did homework. "Put some cheese in that dish!" "Add some sodium to that broth!" "Gimme some love in that cooking!" It was really tough to try and cook without his company.

In the laundry room, I have a tribute from the Western Alliance Rugby team. They put together a collage with photos of Tyler's great plays; the first and only year he played rugby, his team voted him most valuable player. He was fifteen years old, 6'2" tall, and 215 pounds of athletic ability, already playing with nineteen-year-old guys.

Our laundry room doubles as a workout room. In it, Angela painted *Go Big or Don't Go at All*, one of Tyler's mottos.

I purchased some wire words for *smile, happiness*, and *believe* and put them in the walls of my kitchen, trying to lift my soul to a higher vibration while preparing meals.

The Purplest

Alec said that I did not shine anymore. He did not like to be around me or at our home. He told me I was always sad. Instead, Alec preferred to go to the home of our friends, the Gargs.

The Gargs are a beautiful East Indian family of four brilliant girls and two extremely successful parents. They are very, very close to us. They love our children like their own, and vice versa. The Gargs were in Europe when Tyler died. They could not come to his funeral. Rajiv is the father and a long-time friend of our family. The anniversary of Tyler's celebration of life memorial falls on Rajiv's birthday, July 5. He told me he is honored to share this day with Tyler.

Alec spent many days with the Gargs after Ty died. They are his other family.

Who Do You Love the Most?

One day, Alec told me that he thought that I loved Tyler more. I told him, "No, Alec. I just miss Tyler more."

Alec and Ty often competed for my attention and affection when they were little. I purchased a children's book to read to them, *I Love You the Purplest,* by Barbara Joosse.

The book tells the story of a mother of two boys who are always competing for her love. She is always finding a way to love each one uniquely. At the end of the story, each son asks the mother who she loves the most. The mother responds, telling one son she loves him the reddest and the other son she loves him the bluest.

Together, Alec and I read *I Love You the Purplest* for the first time in years. I tried to explain to Alec that I loved him and Tyler differently, but equally. I said, "I could love you the bluest and Tyler the reddest."

Alec responded, "No, Mom. You don't get it! You love me the purplest."

Purple is the highest vibration color connected to divine spiritual realms.

Eleven-Eleven

The numbers eleven-eleven began showing up a lot in my life. I would look at the clock, and it was 11:11. I would make a purchase and the receipt would be for $11.11 or e-mail a digital file and the size would be 1111. Or a license plate in front of me would be 1111. An address, a telephone number, would appear with 1111 in them. It happened so often that I researched the number. It absolutely stunned me to discover millions and millions of hits on the Internet.

The eleven-eleven phenomenon is defined as synchronicity or meaningful events. The sites I took time to browse explained that millions of people are seeing 1111 and feeling something when they do. So many people are experiencing eleven-eleven that it is being described as a spiritual awakening, a conscious evolution. Many people center their thoughts when they see eleven-eleven, believing it will manifest like a prayer or making a wish.

Big Brother

Alec was very lonely for his big brother. One day, forlorn, he asked, "Mom, who's going to stick up for me? Who's going to watch out for me? Who's going to be my role model?"

My heart aching for him, I said, "Honey, who watched out for Tyler and stuck up for him? He was a pretty great guy. So are you."

Inside, I worried over the same thing: *Who was going to protect and guide Alec the way Tyler did?"*

I looked at the clock; it was 11:11 a.m.

The doorbell rang. In walked Dan, a delightful young man. Dan and Ty became good friends in high school. Dan's little brother, Billy, had drowned as a toddler. Dan and Alec understood each other.

Dan walked into our home with purpose, straight for Alec. He said, "I'm here for you, Bud. Let's go throw the football."

The summer of Ty's death, Dan frequently came for Alec. They'd go off together for an hour or two. Alec would come home tired from exercise and happier.

SOLace

At one point, I asked Alec what I could do to help him cope better. He said he wished that there could be a concert or something to honor Tyler. He told me he would like to have a portrait painted of Tyler. I'm convinced Heaven heard Alec's request.

Out of the blue, one of Ty's closest friends, Dan, phoned and asked if he could stop over and get a photo of Ty because he wanted to paint an acrylic portrait. It is a beautiful portrayal of Tyler with a rainbow over his head as if Ty were the sun in our sun rainbow. It hangs in my office next to Angela's sun rainbow art.

Watercolor painting of Alec and his big brother, Ty

A few months later, our middle school art teacher, and my dear friend Pamela, gave a lovely picture of Ty and Alec frolicking in the water to a local watercolor artist. He painted a magnificent portrait of the two brothers laughing it up.

Dan's Rainbow portrait of Tyler

Walking on Sunshine

Fallen Heroes

A few weeks after that, I was reminiscing about Ty and President Eisenhower. Ty was a history buff, and President Eisenhower was one of his personal heroes.

That evening, I was trying to prepare a simple dinner with the television on. A news report was airing the story of a young Minnesota soldier who died in Iraq. I sent a prayer out to the family, still numb with grief over Tyler's death.

The reporter was telling the story of the Michael G. Reagan Portrait Foundation. Michael Reagan is a renowned artist who lovingly creates beautiful, breathtaking portraits of America's fallen heroes at no cost to families.

Michael is described as a gifted artist who possesses a state of grace. I believe that when Michael draws these portraits, the spirit of the soldier is there to help him get it right. Michael is connected spiritually with the souls of these soldiers. The eyes tell. I felt it. On the Fallen Heroes website, the ability to sense the spirit or consciousness in another realm is described as "hollow bone" in Navajo.

Grabbing a piece of paper, I jotted down the artist's name and the website.

The first sentence on the website is "What if all you had left of a loved one was photos and memories?"

I phoned. Michael picked up the call. We talked. I explained that I wanted to commission a portrait of Tyler to honor him and help soothe his brother's grief. Michael told me that he rarely, if ever, picks up the phone. It was very unusual for us to connect.

He explained to me that his nonprofit foundation honors American soldiers by creating a memorial for the soldier's family at no charge. He told me that he is a professional artist, and his work is commissioned for thousands of dollars, including portraits of famous actors, athletes, and presidents.

I explained to him that in Tyler's heart, he was representing America in Japan. I also told Michael that Ty is a hero at his high school for single-handedly reporting a bomb threat and a hero in our hearts because Ty was so passionate about global peace by creating strong relationships overseas.

Michael asked me to e-mail him several photos of Tyler for consideration. I sent something like twenty or thirty digital images with a hope and a prayer. About a week later, Michael agreed to do a portrait of Tyler on his own time as the spirit moved him, for a fee that was within our reach.

Fallen Heroes portrait of
Dwight D. Eisenhower and Tyler Hill
by Michael Reagan

Grateful

Following is a segment of the thank you letter I wrote to Michael:

Everyone who sees the incredibly beautiful Fallen Hero
portrait you created in honor of our sixteen-year-old son,
Tyler Hill, and his personal hero, President General Dwight
D. Eisenhower, is moved emotionally and spiritually. The
warmth! The love! Oh, my God, their faces! We feel them!
And it feels almighty GOOD!

Ty had longed to serve in the military, but knew it would
not be possible because of his diabetes. In his heart, he felt
that the trip to Japan would be a wonderful way to honor
President Eisenhower. We had never seen him happier.

We received notice that the portrait would be available at
the post office the next day. 1111 has spiritual significance to
me. We had to wait in anticipation and honor "Fallen
Heroes" on 11/11/2008—Veteran's Day!! Your portrait
arrived with surreal timing.

I sent you a number of photos to capture Ty's spirit. I
thought you would choose the one where Ty wrote in Japa-
nese script "Eternal Love." The one you selected is the one
we cherish most. This portrait is in our living room in a place
of honor. Ty's face is life-sized. I often humbly kneel before
this picture, look into his eyes, and kiss his paper lips.

There is not enough gratitude in the words thank you.

Michael's rendition of Ty with President Eisenhower has been
reproduced with permission. It hangs in some prominent places of

honor at senate and congressional offices, schools, courthouses, and homes.

This portrait is becoming a hallmark for international travel safety and Depart Smart. Depart Smart is a non-profit organization my family founded to make travel awesome in life-saving ways. Depart Smart provides Travel Hero Safety certification at TravelHeroes.org to help you and those you love "Depart Smart" with an action plan. Most people cannot pass the simple 10-point travel safety quiz on DepartSmart.org. Help us help others with a tax-deductile donation on our website, www.DepartSmart.org.

Michael Reagan's *Fallen Hero* fifth-edition poster includes Tyler and President Eisenhower. If you love someone who died serving America, send photos of your hero to Michael Reagan at Fallen Heroes. Let him use his spirit to connect your hero in his works of art. It's his gift.

My heartfelt intentions for my personal American hero were answered on November 11, 2008, 11/11/08, eleven-eleven, Veterans Day, by divine intervention. Feel the love.

Brothers

Our family began a tradition of taking a ski trip to Park City, Utah, every year during winter break. We would rent a condo near the Deer Valley gondola. We would wake up, eat breakfast, and be on the slopes daily for fun, skiing as a family.

Often, Ty and Alec would split off and ski tree trails, while Allen and I went for steeper groomed runs. Alec was still in middle school the first year we went. Tyler and Alec had memorized the runs to get back to the gondola by the end of the day: Big Stick, Little Stick, Deer Hollow to the Deer Crest lift, and down Jordanelle.

After skiing, we would eat a dinner grilled on the deck and soak in the hot tub under starlit skies. These are awesome memories.

On New Year's Eve, I would make a favorite peppercorn-steak dinner. We would sit around the table, light candles, and talk about ways we could resolve to be better persons, a happier family, sharing our wishes and goals and giving back to others.

Brothers

Only Child

The year Tyler died, I decided to continue the tradition. Allen, Alec, and I went to Deer Valley. We stayed in a different condo, but within the same complex. Alec skied many of the runs he and Ty loved, alone. We offered to ski with him, but he needed his space. He was twelve. We felt close to Tyler at Deer Valley and felt lonely as well.

At dinner on New Year's Eve, Alec was distraught. After dinner, I prepared for our candle tradition. Alec told us he wasn't doing the candles. He said, "I never wanted to be an only child."

We had a very long tear-filled talk about how all of us miss Tyler, wishing things were different.

Global Family

Allen and I hosted four international au pairs when the boys were very small—Sari from Finland, Sylvie from France, Caroline from Sweden, and Gilly from South Africa. Gilly lived with us for more than six years, earning her degree at Crown College.

Gilly revisited us twice the same June Ty died. She traveled from South Africa, once to spend time with all of us and then a second time for his funeral. The morning of her first departure, Ty told her when she hugged him good-bye, "I love you, Gilly. You are going to find your dream job and your dream guy."

She received a phone call shortly after arriving for Ty's funeral that she had indeed received an offer for a prestigious job. She met her husband the year after Ty's death. They are now happily married.

Ty knew. Ty shared a photo of Gilly with his Japanese family. He told them she was his sister in South Africa.

Foreign

Allen suggested that perhaps we could host a foreign exchange student. It seemed like a workable option. Allen commented that we were like a three-legged table, off center and wobbly. A fourth person would round out our family and create a more normal life for us, although it would never be the same as having Tyler in our lives.

That was New Year's Eve, 2007, about six months after Ty died. Alec liked the idea of being an American brother to an international exchange student. I liked the idea of cooking and shopping for four again. We talked about how the school year had already started. We surmised it would be unlikely that a student was available to join our family or that an agency would place a student in a family whose son and brother had died six months earlier. We promised to check into it.

A Brother from Tyler

We arrived back home from Utah a few days later. Mail was stacked high, and the message light indicator was blinking. One message was from Marilyn with the Youth for Understanding (YFU) exchange program. She said she had heard we were interested in a foreign exchange student and needed a family for a young man from Germany rather quickly.

I looked at Allen quizzically and asked if he had made a phone call. He said he had not.

I asked Alec, and Alec said, "No, Mom, we were in Utah."

The following morning, I returned Marilyn's call, confirming that we were very interested in hosting an international student. I asked her how she got our name and number. She asked me to hold on. She returned, crying and audibly upset on the phone. She apologized. She said she should have known that we were Tyler's family and would not have contacted us had she realized.

I said, "It is okay, Marilyn. We are interested. We are still grieving and sad, but we have a lovely home and enough love for another person in our family. I would just like to know how you got our name and number."

Marilyn said, "I have goose bumps, Sheryl. I checked the application. Tyler signed you up to host a student last May."

That May was about four to six weeks before Ty died. Marilyn and I cried. We laughed. We talked about divine intervention. The timing of our family's discussion on New Year's Eve and her outreach to us were uncanny.

Marilyn told me about Nikita, a Russian-born student, raised in Germany, and how he needed a new family by Friday. He was open to being our host son, but needed us to know that he could not replace Tyler. Of course, we already knew that.

Marilyn came by the same evening to review our home, inspect spare bedrooms, complete background checks and paperwork, get recommendations, and expedite procedures.

Allen and Alec were going to a Green Bay Packers football game. I was alone in the house, preparing for Nikita, our German son and brother for the next six months. Tearfully, but with gratitude, I went through Tyler's room and sorted through his things: keep, donate, or give away. I buried my nose into his pillow and packed it away in a plastic bag, hoping to preserve the scent. (That didn't work. The pillow took on the smell of the plastic.)

Tyler's closest friends had already selected something of Tyler's to keep. Ty's cousin could wear his size-fourteen shoes, long pants, and shirts. Most of Tyler's clothing had already been moved. Tyler's life was being boxed away in containers.

NRG

I found Ty's science notebook folded back on a shelf in his room. Ty had abbreviated *energy* as NRG over and over again. Those capital letters stood out on the page of his notes. I felt Ty's NRG and love very powerfully as I prepared his room for Nikita, the host son and brother Tyler had arranged for us in advance.

I upgraded Ty's room with a new dresser and nightstand, bought a desk, a chair, a lamp, and new bedding. It was different, but still an honored space. Ty's sun mural was still on the wall, his iron bed still in the room, the walls his golden yellow.

Once Nikita joined our family, none of us would be lying down on Tyler's bed, grieving for him. Those days ended with Nikita's arrival. It was a good thing.

Brothers

New Brother

I picked Nikita up at the airport that Friday and brought him home. He was a very good eater, athletic, and a smart student with a good sense of humor. With love, we still joke about what a handsome, yet arrogant, young man he is.

Nikita has six-pack abs that he earns and models well.

Nikita is an only child. It took him a few weeks to get used to being a big brother. We had to teach him that it was okay, indeed expected, that he would tease and wrestle with Alec and return brotherly purple nurples (a.k.a. titty twisters).

We had an awesome six months together. Nikita graduated with A honors. We had a very sad farewell. We Skype so that he can practice his English and I can see his pearly white smile and handsome face.

The experience was so positive that we chose to host again, three more times. We have four international sons and brotherly love for Alec from Tyler—and from Germany, Japan, Chile, and Brazil.

Our Japanese YFU son and brother, Yusuke, passed the entry exam into Kyoto University, a very high honor. His family showed appreciation to us by hiking Mt. Fuji on Ty's nineteenth birthday, taking photos with a memorial bandana his school distributed during a tree-planting memorial ceremony. Yusuke will undoubtedly make the world a better place.

Our Chilean YFU son and brother, Roberto, was named Calculus Most Distinguished Student in Mound, Minnesota. Someday he will be a phenomenal engineer or doctor, hitchhiker hair included.

Our Brazilian YFU son and brother, Joao, is closest in age to Alec. They were friends and spent endless hours in each other's company. Joao also achieved a healthier weight, losing twelve pounds playing

Yusuke's family
with Walking on
Sunshine bandana

USA soccer—more strength training than his home school in Brazil. Joao is an affectionate bundle of love. He called me Mom and wrapped me in big-boy hugs. He graduated with honors before he returned home to Brazil.

We love them all, our exchange student sons who became brothers for Alec because Ty signed us up with divine forethought. We love you all the way to eternity, Buddy, forever.

DNA

In the autumn following Ty's death, we received two letters from the Kyoto Eye Bank. They were gratitude letters from the recipients of Ty's corneas.

New Eyes

The first letter was from a relatively young Japanese grandmother who had never seen her grandchildren. She described seeing their smiles for the first time, through tears, because she knew her happiness was our sadness. I wanted her to know that it was not our generosity, but Tyler's, that made her sight possible.

Not long after, another letter arrived. This one was written in elegant prose by an artist who suffered with a genetic disorder that had caused blindness in the left eye when the artist was a teen, and the right eye more than a decade later. The artist explained that he (or she) is an internationally renowned architectural artist. The artist wrote that everything created from here forward would be seen through the beautiful cornea of our loved one. The artist spoke of the sacrifice made for his (or her) own gain and humility. It was a beautiful love letter.

Walking on Sunshine

Watercolor painting by the artist recipient of Tyler's cornea

DNA Memory

Tyler created a MySpace page before going to Japan. He wanted an easier way than e-mail to socially connect with friends and family. On MySpace, he described the one place he would most like to visit, Greece. Remarkably, the Japanese artist created a painting through Ty's cornea for us. The art is not signed for patient privacy reasons.

In Atwater's *The Big Book of Near-Death Experiences*, the author presents some compelling evidence that DNA has memory. The book describes recipients whose lives have been improved through organ transplants as taking on character traits of the donor. If that's accurate, the two Japanese recipients are two very lucky souls. They probably have an unexplained craving for cheese, are deeply affectionate, athletically enabled, tenderhearted, humorous, and spiritually gifted.

Ty, being the generous young man he was, got his wish. Someone else lives a better life because he was here. I checked the donor box on my driver's license. Have you?

Retinitis Pigmentosa

ummer 2011 marks the fourth summer closer to where Tyler's soul thrives. Every day we live is closer to where Ty is. We are all giving up a bit of our health every day, toward the journey to life ever after. Death, like birth, is filled with pain and suffering. I presume that when we suffer our death, we are reborn into eternal life, splendor, and paradise. It's worth it.

In Japan, our Japanese exchange student's family hiked Mt. Fuji with yellow memorial bandanas imprinted with a sun and the words *Walking on Sunshine*, T. Hill, and Japanese *kanji,* or symbol, for love. They took photos of themselves in front of Mt. Fuji and e-mailed them to us. For the past three years, Mt. Fuji has emerged from the clouds on June 6. Such an act of kindness never goes unnoticed.

Geranium

yler's Japanese host mom's birthday is one day after his birthday. For Shigemi, I wanted to create an acrylic painting of her favorite flower, a geranium. I learned weeks later by chance that a geranium symbolizes a true friend and folly. She and I are Japanese soul sisters for life. Destiny.

She is a very fun and outgoing person who cultivates happiness with her spring-fed personality. Concurrently, she is compassionate with heartfelt renderings of a son lost, similar to me. She and her husband tell me that when Ty died, they felt like they lost their son, even though they had only known for a few days.

Shigemi and her family came to visit us a few months after my mom passed. Shigemi came to visit again this year. Both times, she left happy Japanese toys, such as a fragile wooden origami windmill and snacks beside Tyler's crypt to soothe his soul. It was a beautiful act of respect and love.

The day I was painting for Shigemi, Allen asked me to take a boat ride with him because summer is so short in Minnesota. I told him I needed to finish the geranium for Shigemi, and perhaps he could take Alec and leave me behind this one time. I rarely, if ever, refuse a boat ride.

Disgruntled but obliging, he went on without me. Focusing my attention on the art at hand, I deliberately pressed on to create my best possible geranium for Shigemi in time to ship it to Japan before June 7.

As I was engrossed and totally concentrated on my creativity, my cell phone dinged an e-mail message. I picked it up to see if it was Allen or Alec with a final plea for me to join them. I was feeling a tad guilty and ready to relent.

Retinitis Pigmentosa

Blindness

The message was from Shigemi in Japan, wrought with despair. Her son and Ty's exchange brother was attending university to become a dentist. He noticed that his vision was narrowing and went for an exam. He was diagnosed with retinitis pigmentosa.

This is a disease where pigment surrounds the retina over time, creating tunnel vision or potentially complete blindness. Shigemi was grieving for the sight that her son might lose. She was suffering. She asked me to help with American doctors. I did the only thing I knew I could do.

Placing my painting on hold, putting the brushes in a jar of water, settling into a quiet chair, I released the negative energy to the earth like gravity, making the earth stronger. I relaxed my body, my mind, and breathed deeply. I began meditating with a purpose. "Bless Shigemi. Bless her son. Send divine providence for healing."

I don't know how long I meditated. At some point, I had an image of an article replaying in my mind. "Limited release of glaucoma medication in trial study in Tokyo, Japan, to arrest retinitis pigmentosa."

Trusting the divine, I opened my eyes, went to my laptop and typed the text into a search engine. I was gloriously surprised with correct hits! I read about UF-021, a product named Ocuseva for retinitis pigmentosa, being tested in a limited study in Tokyo, Japan. Praises! Holy Lord! It would be within reach in the next year or two.

I copied and pasted the article, which had a link embedded to a site written in Japanese. I realized Shigemi was probably stressing out, unable to sleep, so I phoned her. She answered apologetically for worrying me while grateful to hear my voice. I, on the other hand, was exuberant.

There are tens of thousands of Japanese people in Tokyo who suffer from retinitis pigmentosa. It is a genetic disorder with a strong prevalence toward siblings. Shigemi had good reason to worry about her daughter's vision as well. Tokyo is an ideal geographic location for a clinically controlled release of a medication to arrest the disease. Tokyo is one the most highly concentrated populations in the world. Unfortunately, the city has a cluster of patients with this condition.

Crane

Exuberant with promise of this divine revelation, I finished my geranium painting for Shigemi. I mailed it to her in time for her birthday on July 7. By accident, some weeks later, I learned that the geranium also symbolizes the crane, honor, and loyalty.

Tyler had folded a crane on his trip to Japan that returned in his luggage. He and his group toured Hiroshima. They learned about Sadako Sasaki, who was two years old when America dropped the atomic bomb on Hiroshima, Japan, in 1945. Like so very many, Sadako developed leukemia. She believed that if she could fold one thousand paper cranes, her wish for healing would come true.

Paper was scarce. She created some extremely tiny paper cranes that are smaller than my pinky fingernail. We saw them when we toured Japan, remembering Ty on his seventeenth birthday. Sadako died at the age of twelve. She had folded less than seven hundred, but a thousand paper cranes journeyed with the body that clothed her soul.

Retinitis Pigmentosa

Wishes Come True

Sadako's soul lives on. Every year, schools send thousands of paper cranes to Hiroshima, where they are displayed in a memorial for her. I like to believe that she and Ty are in the light, helping so many more than they ever could on earth. I believe, wholeheartedly, that they helped Shigemi and her son.

I am so very proud of Tyler. At Hiroshima, he knelt by the Japanese Memorial to honor the many who had died crying, "Water, please, water." Many come and leave water at the memorial to honor those who died of thirst after the dropping of the A-bomb. I love you, Buddy!

Sadako and Ty are very busy in the light. Shigemi's son and others have so much hope to arrest blindness. Perhaps some of us are technically blind. Perhaps some who are blind have truer vision.

Tyler, humble and respectful, kneeling at Hiroshima

Incidentally, the crane is considered the symbol of peace and the sun god, Apollo. That resonates for me. Who knows what the divine intends? Here is a photo of the acrylic geranium I finished just in time for Shigemi's birthday. I love you, Shigemi. You are my Japanese soul sister. I know Ty is shining in the light because we are close, because he was here. Feel the love!

Acrylic painting of a geranium for Shigemi Yajima,
Tyler's Japanese host mother

Raging Grief

eturning to the summer Ty died, everything in my home reminded me of him: the place where he sat, the last towel he used, his huge size-fourteen shoes sitting by the garage door, the cheesy foods that he liked to eat. What now?

Numb

It was difficult to shop, cook, do laundry, run errands, any number of things that occur mindlessly in a normal day, but nothing was normal. My brain is trained to think in fours. Four to shop for, to cook for, to clean for, until tragically, we were three.

Ty wouldn't be at the table tonight. He would not eat food enough for two. He would not free sample my cooking when I was not looking. He would not pick me up in a bear hug and refuse to let me go until I told him I loved him. He would not be giving his brother rooster rubs, purple nurples, or secret handshakes. They would never sneak into each other's rooms to talk late into the night again. They would never again go to their fort.

I couldn't cook for months. Ty was not home to shower twice a day, grabbing a clean towel each time. The laundry was half what it used to be. I felt like half the mother. I spent the majority of my day trying to catch my breath, to ease the heaviness in my chest. Lead.

It is not my experience that time heals all wounds. It's been five-plus years. I still miss him. It hurts like a double-edged sword cutting on the way in and on the way out with each agonizing reality. I try not to go there. It hurts to touch that place. It can't be helped. One thought and my stress hormones are on overload.

Enraged with nothing to punch, I confess that I turned to alcohol more than once for pain relief. I'm not the only mom to take a sedative or one too many glasses of wine after her child died. I'm better now. I still miss him.

I Swear

One evening, gripped by despair, I walked outside so that my sobbing would not wake up Allen or Alec. The farther I got away from the house, the harder I cried. In helpless rage, I stomped my foot, raised my fists to the starry Heavens, and cursed God.

"How dare you take my son from me! Do you think you could hurt me any more than this? I thought you were love!" There were a few expletives in there that I will not repeat.

Spent, exhausted, wrought with anguish, I collapsed on the wooden slats of the dock, trying to breathe and slow the heaving in my chest. I waited for lightning to strike me. It didn't.

Divine Voice

I wiped the tears from my eyes and looked up. I felt the Divine speak to me.

"Do you feel better now? My son also suffered and died. Your son is in the light of my son. Trust."

A shooting star shot across the sky and then another, forming a Heavenly cross. The wonder of it was tranquilizing.

I slept right there, in the middle of the night, on the dock. I was so empty and brokenhearted and then a direct connection to Heaven gave me healing relief.

Spirit Healing

A few days later, in the summer of 2007, a close friend phoned me at home. Peggy is a very bright, loving mother of three. She told me that she wanted to take me to a spiritual healer, Vicki, who is not a psychic, but has helped other friends who were also suffering from the death of a loved one.

Spirit

Peggy said she kept having a repetitive thought. "Call my mom. Call my mom." She interpreted that as a message from Tyler to reach out to me. I was reluctant, but I went. I was in horrid anguish.

We arrived at Vicki's. I walked into her home to a cacophony of dogs gone wild, barking. She said they would calm down once we began. They did.

I Feel You

I asked Vicki what the scent was in her house. It smelled of eucalyptus, like a lotion Ty used. She held a frankincense candle to my nose. It wasn't even close to what I smelled.

Vicki said, "I saw the beautiful picture of Tyler in the obituary, all that potential, gone. I felt your pain and knew I would be meeting you. You are in so much agony that you are out of your body. I invited my friend to help me. Hope you don't mind. We need to help ground you."

She asked me to sit in a comfortable chair with Peggy next to me. She asked Peggy to hold my hand and comfort me. Vicki was across from me and her friend next to her. Vicki asked me to close my eyes and try to focus on my breathing: slow, deep inhales and exhales. She helped me inhale and exhale, telling me not to go down in my mind to fear, which leads to despair, anger, and hate, but to rise up to sunshine, love, and light where Tyler dwells. Peggy was gently stroking my arm.

My eyes were closed, but I was not sleeping. I was very aware of my surroundings. Peggy told me I was laughing. I had the most amazing vision of Ty. Ty was standing above my head, near the chair. Ty gently stroked my eyebrows and hair.

He kissed me, saying, "Shh, Mom, shh. Peace."

Ty told me, "I am light everywhere, like the sun, all over the Universe. I am able to help so many more people now than I ever could on earth. I am love and light. I was not alone in my hotel room. I was surrounded by angels."

He told me, "I am so proud to be your son. I am proud of you. Life is short. You can do it, Mom. Love Dad. Love Alec. I'll see you soon. I believe in you."

Ty told me Mary would make certain everything was done right. I assumed he was talking about Mother Mary. There was no sadness, no tears, only Ty's love and comfort.

I opened my eyes. It took me a while to be able to move; my body felt so very heavy, almost sedated. I was extremely calm and relaxed for the first time since the dreadful day we learned of Tyler's trauma.

Peggy told me that Vicki could sense Ty's presence. Vicki, her friend, and Peggy said they had never experienced anything like what had just happened. Vicki could tell me a few things that happened in my vision. I found that remarkable. She also understood that Ty's spirit uses the sun as a symbol of his energy near us. That was a remarkable insight as this story unfolds.

An Angry God

I was raised Pentecostal Baptist. The Old Testament is pretty darned clear that I am not to seek out mediums or spiritists who speak to the dead:

> *Let no one be found among you who sacrifices his son or daughter in the fire, who practices divination or sorcery, interprets omens, engages in witchcraft, or casts spells, or who is a medium or spiritist or who consults the dead. Anyone who does these things is detestable to the LORD, and because of these detestable practices the LORD your God will drive out those nations before you. You must be blameless before the LORD your God.*
> —Deut. 18:10–13 New Living Translation

Could I really be evil because my beloved son brought me comfort from the light? I prayed for wisdom, for understanding. I kept waking up with a recurring thought. "Go to the beginning."

I tried to read the Bible from the front, but the more I read, the more I realized I did not love an angry and jealous God who enslaved his people and destroyed them.

Wisdom

In my quest for wisdom, I discovered the ancient codices of the Nag Hammadi Library, available online. Apparently, these Gnostic codices were likely labeled heretic, back in the day when Romans weren't any too kind or forgiving of Christians, annihilating them in a religious holocaust. I often wonder about the relationship of the Roman Catholic Church with "Roman" in its name and heritage, the history of these Gnostic codices, and how "Holy" books in the Holy Bible became holier than others.

"Gnostic" in my layperson mind means I know God. "Agnostic" means I do not know God. "Atheist" means I don't want to know God. God in my mind means the one and only great love, the Divine. Being *religious* means I accept doctrine at face value. Being *spiritual* means I question everything. If I had to throw my hat in a ring to define my faith, I guess I would be spiritually Christ conscious. I rely on calm, quiet meditations.

The ancient Gnostic texts were protected in sealed clay jars hidden in caves during a volatile time when people died so that the texts might survive. It was a time when religions were being defined. I consider it possible that it was about the same time some books were ranked holier than others and made the cut for the Holy Bible. A bible, after all, is a collection of books, a bibliography. Some books written by some apostles are deemed more holy than others written by other apostles? Why? I would like to know.

I appreciate the open publication of the Nag Hammadi Library and the philosophical approach it takes to texts apparently written by Christian disciples and others.

An Angry God

Secrets

The *Secret Apocrypha of John* describes a Heavenly Aeon, which is and was timeless and androgynous, being neither male nor female. It also describes how the Holy Spirit came to be, Sophia, wisdom, who is love and light and resplendent as the sun, Jesus Christ. I'm still trying to decipher the Seth relationship.

In my interpretation, emphasis on *my* interpretation, the God of the Old Testament was born in sin by Sophia without knowledge of the Heavenly Creator of all. This angry Old Testament God made Adam in the image of "the Father," but could not bring Adam to life. Sophia told the Divine Father, and in agreement, she breathed divine breath, wisdom, into Adam because Adam was formed in the image of the Divine Father, who is love.

The angry Old Testament God didn't receive the spark of the divine from Sophia, wisdom, Holy Spirit, and became angry and jealous of Adam. Adam was separated, the male from the female, creating Eve. Eve listened to the angels who told her that there was a God before this God; otherwise, why would God say, "There is no other God before me"? (*She ate of the fruit of knowledge—listening and understanding the words of the angels.*)

It's a very different rendition from the Old Testament scriptures in the "Holy Bible." I never heard anything like this in Sunday school. I am totally in awe of the Divine Father, Holy Spirit, and Jesus Christ in these codices. I rely on meditative prayer for divine wisdom. Not so much written anything, although I do love to see scriptures serve a greater good for a greater whole. It could happen more often.

I do believe we all come to know the glory of the Divine Father, wisdom of the Holy Spirit, and the eternal light of Christ, in perfect timing.

Dead Talk

I speculated that the angry and jealous Old Testament God does not want us to speak with the dead because the truth would reveal itself, unveiling the true love of the Divine Father, Holy Spirit, and Christ in eternal light.

It is interesting to me that Jesus is quoted in the canonized text of John 8:9: "'You do not know me or my Father,' Jesus replied. 'If you knew me, you would know my Father also.'"

Alive in the Light

After reading a good deal in the Nag Hammadi, I had a realization! My deceased son and I were not speaking to each other. My son is alive in the light! Christ spoke to his disciples after he was crucified, died, and was buried. They saw him. He lives! No one in the Holy Bible tagged them spiritists or mediums!

Sparkle

I have a spark of the divine in me. So do you. In my spiritual journey since Ty's transformation, I have discovered a wonderful communion, a direct connection, with the divine during meditation. Christ consciousness. It's powerful and healing. Paul meditated and saw the third Heaven. Many have. Meditating is discussed often in the Bible and other religious texts.

When I pray, I put my intentions toward Heaven. When I meditate, Heaven brings its intentions to me. I've had some miraculous experiences with a direct connection to Heaven. You can, too. Reach for it; it will come to you. Fan the spark that ignites your soul; grow it. It is love. I do not believe there is a place for anger in Heaven. I do not worship an angry and jealous god (*lowercase intended*).

Habakkuk and Malachi

O ne extremely miserable day in August after Ty died, I was literally inconsolable. My husband told me he did not know how to help me. Ring, ring! The electronic tone of the home phone screeched.

Valiant

A llen answered and then handed the portable handset to me. It was a very dear friend, Valerie. The name Valerie incidentally means "to be healthy and strong." Surreal timing for her phone call because she was thinking of me. I was wretched.

She said to me in the most confident and assured voice, "We need to go to church. I am coming to pick you up. Can you be ready?"

I pulled myself together. Limply and tearfully, I got into her car. The first church we attended was just ending services, switching from summer to fall hours. The second church's service was just beginning.

Silver Dollar

We walked into the sanctuary and sat down, though I was still weeping loudly. Valerie gently held my hand. I was trying to keep my tears from flooding and my sobs silent. The screen in front of the congregation read *In God We Trust*. It had a photograph of a silver dollar with President Eisenhower.

I sighed, remembering the gift of the Eisenhower silver dollar our handyman, Mark, had gifted to Tyler on his sixteenth birthday and Ty's trip to Japan. I hold on to that silver dollar even today as if it identifies me with Tyler, Ike, and world peace.

The pastor also spoke of climbing mountains, calling Ty and Mt. Fuji into my mind.

The pastor's sermon was on Habakkuk in the Old Testament. I remember the pastor speaking about how Habakkuk cried out, "Do you not know, Lord? Do you not see? They gather the innocents of nations as if they were cod from the sea and they release them not! They do not revere your name. They revere their own power and wealth."

But God answered, "Write down the revelation and make it plain on tablets and let it herald. I will release the cod from the nets as the innocents of nations." (*Paraphrased by the author.*)

It must have taken a great courage and a great faith for Habakkuk to stand against adversity and mighty power and write his truth. Think Babylon. I would hope that I might be as faithful and courageous.

This sermon came to us in August 2007, about two months after Ty's transition into the light.

It's All Good

A few weeks after the celebration of Tyler's life, his funeral, my in-laws took my remaining family, Allen, Alec, and me, to a retreat at their condo on Lake Pepin, Wisconsin.

Their place is a lovely spot that looks out over a train track onto Lake Pepin. The train comes whistling by with its lonely wail, echoing the weight of its cars. A few weeks after Ty died, my in-laws went to Lake Pepin to recover and be loved by family.

A sailboat floated by with the letters TY on the sail. My in-laws gave us a beautiful print of this sailboat heeling in the sun. It is like a message from Tyler, saying, "I'm here. It's all good."

The weekend we arrived, we were all raw with mortal grief from the human separation from Tyler's body, soul, and love we missed so much. It was a few weeks after the visit with Peggy and Vicki Abernathy, where Ty communicated with us that he was everywhere, like the sun. He was energy all over the universe. He would help so many more now than he ever could on earth.

Malachi Sun

I was telling my sister-in-law, Candace—Candy for short—about my experience with Peggy and Vicki. I recounted my "Why? Why? Why?" mantra. We were talking over lunch as a song, *Blinded by the Light*, played in the background.

She said, "I need to show you the Pepin Art Festival poster for this year." Every year, Pepin has an art festival. Historically, the art posters have been about the Mississippi River loch, paddle boats, famous hotels, trains, Laura Ingalls Wilder, or other historically significant topics.

This year, the poster was a beautiful shrine by B. J. Christofferson. It has a sun in the center over an ocean. Floating on the ocean is a wooden cradle with the infant Christ, a halo around his head. On Baby Jesus, the artist superimposed an orange blanket with white and green clovers. White represents the eternal and green, life on earth. Ty and Alec used to give each other clover leaves for luck. The clover also represents St. Patrick, the Father, the Son, and the Holy Ghost. In very old cemeteries, you often see shamrocks or daisies on tombstones.

In the poster, cod are jumping from the sea and a net is strung on Baby Christ's cradle. To the left is script about Solomon, and behind the sun, Mt. Sinai—also a volcano and spiritual magnet—in black clouds with light emanating from it, and an olive tree, a symbol of peace.

I needed to know more. I bought several copies of the poster and asked the vendor to relay to the artist B. J. Christofferson that I would appreciate understanding the underlying meaning of her sun shrine if the artist would be kind enough to contact me.

2007 Pepin Art Festival poster

Surreal Timing

A about one hour after I went to church with Valerie and listened to the sermon on Habakkuk, B. J. Christofferson did contact me.

I asked what her Pepin sun shrine poster meant. She told me it means whatever it means to me. I said, "No. I think it has a scriptural meaning, and I would like to understand." I told her about the sermon I had just listened to, about innocents of nations being gathered as if they were cod from the sea.

She told me, "No, no. This is a peaceful, loving shrine. There are no cod captured in nets. The cod are free in the sea."

I said, "Yes, but there is a net on Baby Jesus' cradle. The cod were released from the net like in Habakkuk." She denied that, but I told her to go look.

She came back on the phone astounded and said, "You're right."

I already knew that. I have studied this message, like a link to Heaven, and I know the poster intricately. The net on Baby Jesus's cradle had somehow escaped her.

She asked me to hold. She came back to the phone, saying, "Sheryl, I looked at the resource from which I got the sun. It is from a sixteenth-century Christian text on Malachi, chapter 4."

The Day of the LORD

1 "Surely the day is coming; it will burn like a furnace. All the arrogant and every evildoer will be stubble, and that day that is coming will set them on fire," says the LORD Almighty.
"Not a root or a branch will be left to them.

2But for you who revere my name, the sun of righteousness will rise with healing in its wings. And you will go out and leap like calves released from the stall.

3Then you will trample down the wicked; they will be ashes under the soles of your feet on the day when I do these things," says the LORD Almighty.

B. J., Candy, and I met for dinner. B. J. described a mural she made of the same shrine. I asked her to alter it to be more like the original poster. I bought it. It hangs in my office, ever a reminder that the sun of righteousness rises with healing in its wings on the day that the Lord acts. The eternal sun.

Holy Water

For most of my life, I have lived near water. In Anchorage, Alaska, we lived very near the ocean and spent endless hours fishing, clam digging, beach combing, and watching summer solstice sunrises and sunsets within minutes of each other.

In Minnesota, we are fortunate to live on a lake. Glorious sunrises across the bay welcome us each morning. If we are out on the bay, we can watch amazing sunsets over our home. I love being around bodies of water. I would often go down to the dock to cry, pray, meditate, relax my mind, especially after Ty's death and when my mother was dying.

Dr. Emoto

Quite by accident, I was reflecting on the calming peace being near water brings when I happened across a children's picture book, *Messages from Water*, by Masaru Emoto. I was intrigued all the more because Dr. Emoto is Japanese.

In his remarkable book, he tells children that like the Earth, our bodies are 70 percent water. The book has a multitude of photos taken of water crystals formed during a freezing state, explaining that if we play calm music, speak kind words, or place a photo of something near the water, the crystals that form will be beautiful or take a shape similar to the photo.

Conversely, if we play harsh music or speak rudely or use words that are hateful, the crystals will be malformed and devastated. Photos of the crystals demonstrate Dr. Emoto's philosophy. The Internet has examples of Dr. Emoto's *Messages from Water*.

The words "thank you" in Japanese means "to be grateful for your own existence."

Crystal formed with the words "Thank You"

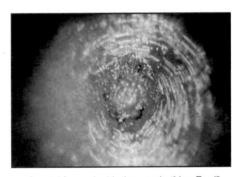

Crystal formed with the words "You Fool"

Rice Experiment

Wanting to believe that our energy, words, and intentions change the molecular structure of water molecules in our bodies, I performed the rice experiment Dr. Emoto describes at the back of the children's picture book.

I bought two baby-food jars, dumped the contents, and sterilized the jars. I cooked up some rice, not paying any particular attention to the type of rice, and filled each baby-food jar. I capped the jars as tightly as possible. On one, I wrote *Hate* and *Anger* with black, waterproof marker. On the other, I wrote *Love* and *Gratitude*. I told my husband and son not to mess with my rice, seriously but with a smile.

Emotions are hard to control when events in your life are out of your control. Tyler's death, wrongful death lawsuit, and my mother's failing health could cascade my emotions into despair.

I took my angry emotions out on the "hate and anger" rice, opening the door to the fridge, picking it up, walking away with the jar, and saying, "I hate you! You're ugly." Afterward, I'd put it back on a low shelf, way in the back of the refrigerator.

Likewise, when I felt loved or happy by a gesture of kindness or good news, I reopened the fridge, took out the "love and gratitude" rice from the opposite corner of the fridge, caressed it lovingly, and spoke, "I love you. I am thankful."

My results paralleled Dr. Emoto's results. My "anger and hate" rice got moldy and soured. My "love and gratitude" rice fermented into yellow, sweet wine vinegar. The results were startlingly different, so different that I keep a red glass inscribed with "Thank You" on my kitchen windowsill to remind me that my thoughts, words, and intentions form the molecular structure of my being. I also keep blue glass jars of water near me, energized by sunlight, reminding me to keep my thoughts and intentions as high as possible.

Grace with Intent

Most everyone understands that stress and anxiety can cause illnesses, headaches, weight gain, high blood pressure, high cholesterol, and more. It shouldn't surprise anyone that our thoughts and intentions can affect our well-being.

Reading *Messages from Water* and performing its experiment placed my mind in a receive mode. I learned deep relaxation and meditation techniques by intentionally seeking out ways to build a better, happier life.

Saying grace used to be something I did because my family did it. Grace has become a more important practice for me. My Grandma Smith used to tell me that the most important ingredient she put in her recipes was love. With intent, love and gratitude are the first ingredients moms use to prepare meals. Try it. Transform your thoughts from despair or frustration into love and gratitude and see manifestations of your heart's desire transform. It happens. It's real.

Thoughts = Deeds

It's not always easy to love. Our thoughts become our words. Our words become our deeds. Our deeds shape our character. Our characters defines our souls. Our souls need to shine.

I believe in righteous anger. Righteous anger calls us into action, motivating us to create change, to right wrongs.

Temperament

My closest friends tell me I am generous and tender-hearted to a fault, but they would never want to make me angry. Fortunately, they tell me it takes a lot to make me angry.

One definition of temper, as in steel, is to bring to a desired consistency. I am learning to temper my temper. I have Irish blood. I am learning to test my temperament to determine if my anger is self-serving or for a greater good for a greater whole. I am still learning.

At the same time, I stand up for what I believe in with an uncannily strong will, hopefully with grace and grit. That strength comes from a source greater than me.

A Tyranny of Words by Stuart Chase mirrors my intent. What is truth? The eye of the beholder can shape it into a self-serving reality. I desire a higher truth. It takes a strong-minded will. We all have free will. Mind it! Please. Perhaps when an angry and jealous god made us, he made us angry and jealous?

Dr. Emoto's messages from water are a constant reminder to me that energy, our intentions, thoughts, words, and deeds shape who we are and our outcomes. Our prayers are enveloped in our thoughts. If you pray for peace, but secretively desire that your troops dominate, which is stronger—the will or the prayer?

Angry Eyes

As a little boy, Tyler once professed to me that it takes ten loves to right one hurt. I believe him. His brother used to tell me not to look at him with angry eyes.

I believe the Divine is loving and forgiving and knows our desire for justice. Amen! So be it. I desperately want to lose the angry eyes.

Prove Holy

I have read that Dr. Emoto has come under harsh scrutiny because he has not proven his philosophy in a double–blind scientific study and sells products based on his claims. So much so that a double blind study was done. The Holy Bible has never proved its holiness in a double-blind study either.

On a spiritual healing retreat to Sedona, Arizona, I went to a chapel on a hill to light candles and pray. Holy water was available at the entrance of the chapel for parishioners. The chapel store sold holy water and oil. I could light a candle for a dollar donation. I bought everything, intending to bless and anoint my dying mother and light candles for loved ones in the light. I never thought twice about scientific evidence that the water and oil in the containers were indeed transformed and holy or the scientific evidence that the candles I purchased for a buck a piece did the trick. It takes faith.

Source

ater is a source of life. We are 70 percent or more water; so is the Earth. Water is often referenced in holy texts. I did a key word search in an electronic New International Version of the Bible. Water appeared six hundred and twenty times. I love a scripture in John where Jesus speaks to the Samaritan woman, saying, "Whoever drinks the water I give him will never thirst. Indeed, the water I give him will become in him a spring of water welling up to eternal life." Whoosh!

Replenishing our bodies with sixty-four ounces of water is the recommended daily dose. I drink water to replenish my body. I bless the water with love and gratitude to replenish my soul. I can't scientifically prove that the water I bless is holy or divine.

Dr. Emoto's rice experiment demonstrated the healing or destructive power of our intentions. I began making a conscious effort to shape my intentions. As I opened up to the possibilities of emotional wellness that conscious intent could bring, my consciousness opened higher.

Into the Dark

Almost immediately after Tyler's tragedy, I was placed on anti-anxiety medicine. Lexapro brought my lows up and my highs low, cause and effect. I wasn't as sad as I could have been, but I wasn't as happy either—numbness. Sometimes numbness is good because you can't feel the pain. Sometimes it is bad because you can't feel pleasure either. I wanted the second half of the equation back. Seriously.

EMDR

My grief counselor worked with me. We tried meditation, thought field therapy, and eye movement desensitization and reprocessing (EMDR). There is a wealth of information from authenticated resources on the Internet about all of the above.

EMDR is effective for post–traumatic stress disorders. EMDR was to suppress the angst and despair of removing Ty from life support. Everyday triggers, like anything Japanese, could catapult me into despair. EMDR was an instrument to suppress the most horrific memory of my life.

Near-Death Experience

It may have done more than that. Atwater's *The Big Book of Near-Death Experiences: The Ultimate Guide to What Happens When We Die* affirmed my experiences explicitly. Atwater states that patients who have undergone EMDR have similar experiences to near-death survivors. Perhaps this and my conscious effort to shape my intentions created my experience.

For years after Ty's death, I have not slept well. I could be busy all day, but the solitude of nighttime engulfed me in monkey-mind thoughts I could not quiet. My thoughts would replay Ty's death and all the events of our life that would never be because he had died. Combine night sweats with grief and the problem is exacerbated. I would lie in bed next to my husband and look at the ceiling.

One night, the ceiling was blacked out by a dark space. It looked like a cloud, a hole, a tunnel, a cave; it was a dark space, however you would like to define it. It moved. It expanded. It came closer. It narrowed. It moved away. I got up in bed and tried to touch it. I woke my husband up shifting around. I asked him if he saw it.

He grumbled, "You're dreaming. Go back to sleep."

I felt an overwhelming sense of rightness when the black space was there. I wanted it back. I closed and opened my eyes, willing it to appear. Finally, I focused on my breathing. I took deep, slow nasal breaths. In with the good, out with the bad, relax your fingers, relax your toes, let go.

Into the Dark

Out-of-Body Experiences

I have read numerous accounts of people having out-of-body experiences (OBE). Mine was so different. I saw the lower half of my body beneath the covers on the bed from the upper left corner of the bedroom, then a dark, peaceful, black space—no worries, no fears. Wisdom and a knowing that was all-encompassing.

I was suddenly surrounded by an amber, ambient light without an identifiable source. It was golden and vibrant. I could feel it. The vibration was Heavenly and healing. Until I read Atwater's book, I would recount my experience as being surrounded by angels. I saw hundreds, perhaps thousands, of what I defined as angel heads making this amazing vibration. How would I know if they are angels? I saw golden haloes. I defined them as angels.

A divine voice vibrated in my soul. I understood that I was to look away from the harmony and bliss. I saw Tyler. He was so very happy and with so many friends whom he loved and who loved him. I was so captivated by the vibration that I wanted to go back to the amber light.

I felt a loving vibration that I understood as "Do you see? Do you know? Go now. Your time is not yet. Write it down. Love." And then I was catapulted back into my body. It hurt.

I felt very heavy, almost leaden. I could not find my fingers or my toes. I could not move. My body was dead weight. Atwater held a discussion where she talked about how people experiencing OBEs stop breathing. I relate.

Tears fell because I did not want to be here; I wanted to go back. Slowly, my soul reconnected with my mind and then my mind to my body. Lethargically, I rolled to the side of my bed, let my feet touch the floor, pushed myself up with both arms, and rested. I took several breaths and stood up, wobbling my way to the bathroom. I switched on the light, then stumbled to the counter and braced myself up. I looked in the mirror.

My face was glistening. It looked like sparkles of amber light were coming from my pores. I rubbed my face and my eyes and looked again. I ran cold water and poured it over my face. As the heaviness left my body, the glistening faded and went away. I was back to this reality. Atwater reports that many have had my experience. I felt relieved after reading that, as I was no longer alone.

Affirmations

I told some very close spiritual friends about my experience, with a caveat: "If you think I am nuts, please get me help." They reminded me that I was already getting help and that I should speak to my psychiatrist and to my psychologist. They thought my experience was divine and told me I was blessed. My psychiatrist was a former Lutheran minister.

They also reminded me that Moses' face sparkled. In Atwater's book, the author recounts numerous people who have had similar encounters; the exception is that they had near-death experiences. I, on the other, had EMDR and wished to leave the horrid pain of Tyler's death behind to find some solace from my fractured heart.

Into the Dark

In my search for understanding the out-of-body experience (OBE), I discovered OBEs are relatively common. One in ten people experience them. Sometimes the experience is brought about in near-death situations. The other most prevalent causes are severe emotional or physical trauma, EMDR, and conscious meditation. Most scientists classify episodes induced by drug use as hallucinations. The experience is also labeled astral projection, spirit walking, or remote viewing.

Remote Viewing

In my search for wisdom surrounding out-of-body experiences, a surprising discovery uncovered remote-viewing research with the United States Defense Intelligence Agency (DIA) within a book titled *Limitless Mind* by Russell Tarq.

From 1969 to the mid-1990s, the DIA engaged in psychic warfare, training and using remote viewers for defense intelligence collection projects. A minimum accuracy of 65 percent was required to stay in the program. Originally named SCANATE ("scan by coordinate"), remote viewing was conducted at Stanford Research Institute. Psychic warfare continued over the next decades under names like Gondola Wish, Star Gate, Sun Streak, and others.

The Federation of American Scientists (FAS) published a report called *Star Gate (Controlled Remote Viewing)*, recounting the history and success of psychic warfare. FAS conducted thousands of remote viewings with success so dramatic they were termed "eight martini viewings" because the results were mind-boggling.

A number of scientific associations have been formed to research and report out-of-body experiences, after-death communication, remote viewing, astral projections, and so on, such as the International Remote Viewing Association and International Association of Near-Death Studies (IANDS).

Before I had my out-of-body experience, I saw a black space above my bed. I have read numerous books, trying to find information from anyone else to validate my experience.

Love

Several accomplished authors and researchers write about how people who have had near-death experiences tell of a life review. It's not always a good experience. They describe feeling emotions they were responsible for causing from the other person's perspective. If the emotions were joyous, with love and gratitude, for example, they enjoyed feeling that. However, if the life review played out suffering, sadness, fear, anxiety, pain, the person felt that intensely and in entirety. In this life review, people judge themselves. They must love and forgive themselves for all the pain they may have caused, or remain in the dark, literally.

In *Bridge Over the River*, a soldier, Sigwart, communicates with his sister after death. The soldier's heart was serving his country, and he died a national hero. The intent was for a greater good for a greater whole, so life reviews of war tragedy appear to me to be forgiving, based on intent.

As I write, the scripture "Forgive, even as I have forgiven you" replays in my mind.

The following is written in 1 Corinthians 13:13: "Faith, hope, love, the greatest of these is love." Perhaps now I understand why love is the greatest; it elevates our soul so we can shine with the eternal sun.

Premonition

A few weeks before his death, Tyler told me that he thinks things and they happen.

I asked him, "Like what?"

He told me, "Like I wanted a black compact car that was good on gas, and you and Dad bought a used Kia for me. Or like my friend Loren will need me, and I get a call. Or like I'm going to have an awesome rugby game and I score three tries." This wasn't the first time Ty conjured up reality with thoughts.

Mind Screams

Once when Ty was five and in kindergarten, newly diagnosed with type I diabetes—before functional insulin treatment—the phones went out in our neighborhood. I had no reason to worry about Tyler, but I could not stop a recurring thought in my mind. "Mommy! Mommy! Come here! I need you."

I went downstairs and started lacing up my shoes when Gilly asked me what I was doing.

I said, "Ty needs me. I am going to his school."

She asked me how I knew that because the phones were out.

I said, "I just know."

When I arrived at the school, I went to check in at the office. The staff looked at me and said, "Oh, thank God!" I saw Ty in the nurse's office. He was pale and gray, experiencing low blood sugar. The school nurse was trying to bring his blood sugar up with a lollipop.

She looked at me and said, "We are trying everything, and nothing is working." I took a juice box out of my purse and put the straw to Ty's lips. He drank. In a few minutes, his eyes brightened.

He said, "Mommy, I was calling you over and over!"

I said, "Yes, baby. Yes, baby, I know. Mommy heard you."

Into the Dark

Alien

One evening, just before Ty's trip to Japan, Ty opened our bedroom door slowly, walked gingerly to my side of the bed, woke me up, and told me he needed to talk to me. He looked worried. He took me by the hand and led me to his room. Remember, Ty was six feet two inches tall and 215 pounds of muscle with a very big heart at fifteen years old.

He said, "Mom! I am so freaked out. I think an alien was in my room at the foot of my bed."

I said, "Ty, have you been watching spook shows again?"

"Mom! No! Serious! I'm freaked out. Stay here."

"Ty, why don't we pray?"

I prayed, "Dear Heavenly Father, whatever angel or saint you sent to Tyler is freaking him out. Please don't do it again. Send your guardian angels to protect him while he rests, but let them be out of sight, hold him close to your light and love. Amen."

Ty has a number of very loving aunts and uncles who are Mormon. One aunt made a long trip from Utah to visit us after Ty died. I told her about the night Tyler got freaked out. She explained to me that Mormons are not so narrow-minded that they believe humans are the only intelligent life-forms in the universe.

Guardians

Ty never described the being that he saw. Dr. Lerma says many patients see angels before they die. If you've ever read the Bible, you know there are some powerful beings in there that are described monstrously. In Ezekiel, seraphim guard wheels of light; within the wheels of light are the spirits of the living beings. Seraphim are considered by some to be the highest, most powerful angel beings. In Ezekiel 10, for example, the following is written:

> *Each of the four had the face of a man, and on the right side each had the face of a lion, and on the left the face of an ox; each also had the face of an eagle.*
> [11]*Such were their faces. Their wings were spread out upward; each had two wings, one touching the wing of another creature on either side, and two wings covering its body.*
> [12]*Each one went straight ahead. Wherever the spirit would go, they would go, without turning as they went.*
> [13]*The appearance of the living creatures was like burning coals of fire or like torches. Fire moved back and forth among the creatures; it was bright, and lightning flashed out of it.*
> [14]*The creatures sped back and forth like flashes of lightning.*

Those beings would scare the wits out of me, but I definitely want them guarding the spirit of my living being in the next place that I go.

Into the Dark

Tunnel

In my search for understanding of the tunnel, dark space, cave, black cloud, or whatever, I found an article on a blog at My Efficient Planet online. The article is titled "The Awesome Powers of Dark Energy and Matter—a New Cosmology?" by Russell Symonds.

The article describes darkness as comprising the majority of the universe, massive voids of ever-expanding space. Dark matter is that expansive space between stars with just enough gravity to hold them together. I imagine a night sky with a dark canvas that magnifies the brilliance of the stars. Like the yin and yang, one is not complete without the other. You cannot have dark without light, and vice versa, you cannot have light without dark. You cannot have the Divine Father without the Holy Spirit. They are interdependent.

Vibration

All matter has a vibration. Perhaps some vibrations cannot be felt with human senses. All matter has atoms and molecules that are constantly moving. Perhaps dark space is that introduction to higher vibrations, where matter as we know it, ceases to exist.

I am no longer afraid of the dark. It is the precursor to the amber, ambient light at the end of the tunnel. It is the womb before Paradise. Death has no meaning there; it is the dark balance of light, love, energy (NRG), and new beginnings in the next place we go.

Sweet as Honey

Yoga

The name Pamela means as "sweet as honey." Pammy, middle school art teacher and certified yoga instructor, is all that her name implies. Pamela coerced me into her evening yoga classes to calm my soul after Ty's death. Yoga trains the consciousness to enter into a perfect state of spiritual insight and tranquility. One fall evening, after learning the art of meditation, I zoned out during child's pose and became a believer. My mind, consciousness, opened as if I were standing among the constellations, one with all—peace, euphoria. Best yoga class yet!

MOPS

Pammy spent endless hours letting me pour out tears and grief into her open heart, crying with me, laughing, sharing, remembering Ty during long walks on a farm, sunset cruises, and dinners out.

Pamela's daughter was involved with MOPS (Mothers of Pre-schoolers) and asked Pammy if she knew someone who was very spiritual to present to her local MOPS chapter. Pamela gave my name, and within a few days, I was on the MOPS calendar to speak a few weeks later.

The MOPS mission statement at that time was "Love as far and wide and deep and high as the soul can reach." The first anniversary of Tyler's death was looming a few months ahead. I prayed, meditated, hoped for guidance to bring a message that could build on MOPS mission.

I spoke about how our children teach us to see beauty close up. They have "faithful innocence." I asked them to watch closely at what captivates their toddler's attention and brings them joy: a dandelion transformed into a love flower, a leaf with its own prints, sunlight refracting through water, and how little people's simple prayers are so powerful. MOPS moms were asked to do a small assignment, sharing lessons they learned from their preschoolers. The responses were awesome.

I told MOPS moms how Ty woke in the night, saying Heaven called his name and that he was going to Heaven, but I couldn't come until later. I told them how he prayed a simple prayer to be a normal little boy with diabetes. When Heaven answered, he was listening. I admitted falling on my knees in helpless exasperation and calling out to God until exhaustion rendered me unable. I asked what they would do if their child told them something similar.

YVHG

There is a book that puts forth the premise that God's name is literally encoded in every human body. According to this book, the basic elements of DNA—hydrogen, nitrogen, oxygen, and carbon—directly translate into specific letters of the Hebrew alphabet (YHVG), which in turn spell out one of the original names of God. Yahweh is the name God told Moses, "I am that I am." Ehyeh Asher Ehyeh.

What if the angry Old Testament God was claiming that he is of the divine All? To me, that God is not the one who manifested the Holy Spirit. Give to Caesar what is Caesar's. Give to God what is God's. Give to the divine All what belongs to the Divine All. If the Old Testament God truly created man from the dust of the earth, he gets the body. It turns to dust. The Divine, the All, who manifested all we know, owns the spark. We shine brighter than the sun in the next place.

Anger Zaps

A fter what I will refer to as my visit to the light, my out-of-body experience, I was stunned back into my body. I wondered what had just happened and why on earth I was still here. I felt awestruck, confused. Back in reality, my life was still upside down. My mind was stuck somewhere in the middle of Heaven and earth. The next two weeks were unreal.

Sprint

T yler had a cellular phone in Japan with an international calling plan that failed to work. There was an attempt to speed dial his dad and one to call service for the carrier. The cell phone was in Tyler's backpack when it returned from Japan. I took the cell phone to the carrier to request a refund. The carrier tried to tell me I was locked into a multiple-year plan. I know I had never signed up for a multiple-year plan.

I wrote a letter to Senator John Kerry for help. He was chairing the Communications Oversight Committee. A few weeks later, I received a telephone call from the carrier's chief executive office, informing me that the contract, which I never agreed to, was cancelled. The carrier would not allow me to return two telephones that cost almost $1,000, however. The carrier was Sprint. Our Minnesota attorney general brought a class action against Sprint shortly afterward. I am not a Sprint fan. I am definitely a fan of federal oversight.

We switched to AT&T, upgrading to iPhones. I kept Ty's Sprint cell phone, but removed its SIM card. Our attorney thought we might need to demonstrate that Ty tried to phone Allen from Japan, but the phone failed. I kept the phone charging on a wall outlet in my office. It had a tendency to ring on its own, without a SIM card, even in our attorney's office.

The dates that Ty's phone rang were bizarre. It rang on our anniversary, at Christmas, and his brother's birthday, for example. The phone would register missed calls, and the voicemail prompt would indicate a message. If I tried to connect to voicemail, the prompt would read, "No SIM card." Maybe Sprint has a phone locator that pings the device, who knows. The dates, however, were random.

Anger Zaps

Zap

Other electronics went wrong around me after my Heavenly visit or out-of-body experience. I could not walk into a department store without setting off the alarm. Speakers would buzz as I walked past. I could not use my iPhone. It would lock up. I could not start my Prius. It would lock up. I ultimately had to replace its battery. I felt electric shocks zap through my body like every synapse was amped up and misfiring. It hurt badly.

I could walk in from the cold winter, and arcs of static electricity would zap the first metal I came within two feet of. It felt like I had just touched an electrical outlet with wet hands.

Pumping gas was scary. I made certain to ground myself on something metal before I got out of the car and before touching the gasoline pump.

A dear friend suggested I go to Spring Forest Qigong Center for energy healing to "ground myself." I did. That same day, I went home, and the light bulbs in my ultraviolet reading lamp exploded, twice. I have to special order replacements for these lamps; they aren't cheap.

I threw mail across the counter. An arc zapped the electronic controls on my gas range. Gas started spewing in the kitchen from all five burners. The starter buttons were not working. I could not shut the gas off. I opened windows and held a lighter wand to the burners to ignite them.

Yusuke, our Japanese exchange student, came to the rescue by removing storage drawers beneath the stove, climbing underneath the counter, and shutting off the gas valve. The stove would have to be replaced.

I used the grill to cook dinner that night. I cooked potatoes in the microwave. When I went to mash them, my electric hand mixer started smoking in my hand. After dinner, I started the dishwasher. It went bonkers and started flooding. Aagh! Almost everything electronic stopped working for me, and repairs were getting expensive. I had no control over the energy (NRG) leaving my body.

NRG Healing

I phoned Spring Forest Qigong and told them what was happening, explaining that I could not live like this. They asked me to go outside and stand on the ground, spread my feet, bend my knees, breathe a holy breath, and hold the energy in my *dantien*, or solar plexus. (Yes, even our body has an energy center defined as SOLar.) I tried. I felt electric shocks traversing my spine and exploding out my tailbone. My younger son was in the kitchen, joking that I was blowing sparks out my rear. I kid you not.

Kundalini

Many months later, I would be describing my experience to a medical professional, who then introduced me to Kundalini. Kundalini is energy stored within our spine that slowly coils like a snake. Her explanation reminds me of the rod of Asclepius, the image of a rod with wings and a snake coiling up used as a symbol of medicine in health care.

Qi is pronounced *chi*. It represents the life energy found in all things. In Chinese medicine, qi balances positive and negative energy and is the source of good health. Qigong is a meditative mental and physical practice for mental health and enlightenment and other mindful practices requiring balance.

I take fifteen to thirty minutes each morning for meditation. My meditation is a connection to a divine trinity for a greater good for a greater whole. I release negative energy to the earth; the earth loves gravity. I breathe in the Holy Spirit, the Divine energy, a limitless power source, and visually store that in my solar plexus next to my heart.

I feel the difference when my day is so rushed I cannot balance; others feel it around me too. I'm not fun. I also meditate during exercise. It is the single most important thing I do for my health.

Divine Power

The Qigong master explained to me that the Divine is love and light. The power of the Divine will not stay within us if we are in despair or anger. I was counseled to breathe deeply, center the Divine energy in my solar plexus reservoir, and let go of anger and despair.

The center asked me to come in early the next day, which I did. Master Lin told me that he had a similar experience in his life and encouraged me to attend his seminar. He said it was a gift. Tearfully, I said I would like to return the gift, because it wasn't working for me.

Master Lin told me he had many masters who would like to be able to have what I have. He said he would help me. That session, I went into a deep meditation, and a very severe arc of electricity went from me to Master Lin or vice versa. He warned me before it occurred. It hurt.

I was volted! I flinched and cried out. He encouraged me to breathe deeply and often, to learn how to meditate deeply, and to let go of anger and fear. He told me to breathe in the limitless love and energy of the Divine, to forgive, to love, and to use this love and energy to serve and heal others. I try.

Meditate or Medicate

I personally have not taken a Qigong course. I did read Master Lin's books and learned butterfly breathing and centering energy during meditation. Perhaps someday I will take the next step. There is only one letter difference between medication and meditation. Personally, I prefer the latter.

When Heaven gives you a gift, you're supposed to share it. I'm still trying to figure out how to share this one.

Tyler Evidence

A tough lesson to learn is that just because things are terrible does not mean that they cannot get worse. I was barely coping with my dad's death when Joshie and Sherry were killed by a drunk driver.

Worse and Worse

A few months after Ty died, the husband of one of my best friends, Denise, fell off his roof and died. Then, my mother's physician informed me that severe stress can cause dementia to worsen rapidly. My mom was to be placed on hospice care as she neared the end of her life. Simultaneously, we were finalizing a legal complaint for Hennepin County Court. The holidays were also just around the corner, lurking with a painful reminder that Ty would not be celebrating with us. And then I discovered that someone had pilfered my iTunes account for more than $1,500.

Closing the shades to my room, I tried to circumvent a full-scale annoying and painful headache by resting for a while. I recalled a book

I had recently read, titled *Left to Tell* by Immaculee Ilibagiza. It described the horrors of Rwanda's genocide war with Tutsi and Hutu neighbors—people the author had gone to school with and relied upon. I tried to put myself in a place where my distraught pain was nothing by comparison.

I repeated a mantra in my mind: "I am so blessed. I have a lovely home. I live in a supportive community. We have good schools. I have a wonderful husband and Alec. I love America. I love my husband. I love Alec. I am grateful for my time with Tyler. Why, Buddy? *WHY? WHY? WHY?* I wish I knew the truth about how you died."

Always Here

I felt the bed compress next to me. I heard Tyler's voice, and then I saw him like a hologram projection. He was leaning over me. His hand was resting on the bed beside me, near my hip. He was bigger than life. He said, "Mom, did you read what happened the night before I got really sick?"

I said, "Yes, baby. I did. We all did. Why?"

He said, "You need to get up and go read it again."

"Why, Honey?"

"Just do it, Mom."

I sat up in bed, and he was gone. I moaned and cried and began to shake. I called out, "Don't leave me, Ty. Don't leave me!"

I felt a vibration; I understood him. "I'm not, Mom. Love never dies. I am always, always, right here."

I wailed. Crying, sobbing, shaking, trying to breathe. I held the walls for support while I wandered into my office. I went through emotional times, dealing with evidence that made me relive Tyler's death.

With wrenching sobs, I reached for the phone and called my attorney. Through disjointed phrases, I gasped out my vision of Tyler. After decades of experience in wrongful death lawsuits, he was not the least bit surprised.

In my heart, I know without a doubt that Heaven sent my son to answer my plea. "Why? Why? Why!"

What I learned is not as important as the fact that Tyler helped me understand why. More importantly, I learned that love never dies. Tyler's love is always with me.

Sun Rainbow

A very short month after Tyler's funeral, Alec and I tried to surprise Allen on his birthday with the surprise dinner cruise Tyler had helped plan. We placed a paper bag over Allen's head as we walked up to the boat. The three of us were wearing yellow Walking on Sunshine shirts, as were most of the friends and family on the boat.

One of Ty's schoolmates, Dan, was the captain of the boat, the same friend who showed up at 11:11 a.m. to take Alec out to toss a football when Alec worried about who would watch out for him.

Walking on Sunshine

Allen, Alec, and I were trying to be stoic as we walked toward the restaurant to check in. It was hard. This was the party Ty dreamed up. Abbey, Ty's girlfriend, was following behind us.

She took a snapshot of our backs because she said she saw an incredible rainbow around us. I didn't see the photo until several weeks after the party when Abbey e-mailed it to me. I was mesmerized.

There is a brilliant white sun beneath an iridescent rainbow above us. A green sphere of light was touching all three of us with a shape inside of it. The photo, for me, symbolized the promise of life after death, eternal light, and wisdom. There was so much love surrounding us that day.

Sun Rainbow—one of many divine interventions

I love this sun rainbow photo so much I asked an artist, Angela L., to paint it in the upper left corner of my home office. Angela and I became great friends. She gave me a book by Alan Ames, *Through the Eyes of Jesus.*

Several months later, Angela and I went to a mystic Catholic mass with Alan Ames, who is internationally known for his healing ministries. We went forward to be blessed ourselves, and also held photos of loved ones to be blessed. After communion, we went to a book signing where Alan Ames would sign our copy of *Through the Eyes of Jesus.*

I shared the sun photo with the author. He took one look at it and said, "Yes, this is the Host. Here is the Father, Son, and Holy Spirit." I asked him to explain.

He said, "The Holy Spirit is represented as the rainbow, our Heavenly Father as the sun." Alan took the photo from me and turned it upside down, saying casually, "In the green light, the most holy prayer, the Eucharist."

I saw it then. Inside the green sphere of light is an image of a Holy Grail emanating from the sun, with the sacrament shining as bright as the sun.

Months later, I found a scripture in Revelations describing the throne of Jesus Christ as if a light were shining through an emerald. I think of Ty in the light with the Trinity: *I will make you like a morning star. Your face will shine like the sun. I am the light of the world.*

I've been back to that spot on the same date, at the same time, every year. The sun just doesn't line up. I keep thinking it will. The sun is higher in the sky at seven o'clock in the evening. It sets more to the right of us across the bay. There is a big brown house shaded by very large trees that block the view. I have taken numerous photos and cannot recapture the rainbow sun.

It is the same photo I shared with Dr. Lerma after reading his book *Learning from the Light,* which describes iridescent rainbows with golden spheres of light that fill the room as people pass away.

Full-Spectrum Light

Several weeks after I shared the photo with him, Dr. Lerma wrote to me, "Rainbows are the full spectrum of what creates visible light. We know that around that visible light spectrum are other invisible energies or light. Some are the gamma rays and X-rays. They are so intense and likened to the sun. God is pure energy with love, righteousness, and justice at its core."

I do believe him. I have seen this light in Merkabah in so many, many photos.

Merkabah

Interdimensional Vehicles of the Soul

In October following Tyler's death, my dear friend's husband also died. At the time I learned of his death, I had commissioned an artist, Angela (that really is her name), to paint the sun rainbow photo on my office wall. I needed the sun rainbow in the left corner. Though I did not know it at the time, Dr. Lerma stated that often angels appear in the left corner near the ceiling.

Angela phoned me to say that she craved cheese balls the entire time she was painting the sun rainbow in my home office. I told her Ty loved cheesy foods. We laughed.

She also told me that she had needed a fan to quickly dry the paint so she could apply sparkles to the sun. She asked Ty where to find a fan. She said she knew instinctively where the fan was in our house and walked right to it in a small storage area within our garage.

Then, she tried to explain to me that there was a sun in a picture of the sun rainbow that she painted on my wall. I said something like, "Isn't there supposed to be? That's what I asked you to paint."

She said, "No. There is another sun in the sun rainbow picture. I'll have to show it to you."

However, there was a funeral to plan and attend. It would be several weeks before Angela and I would reconnect on the sun rainbow painting and final acceptance. Angela came to my home. She showed me a copy of the picture she took of the wall art of the sun rainbow. There, in the middle of the photo, in broad daylight, without a flash, was the first appearance of Merkabah, an interdimensional vehicle of the soul, described in Tyler's spirit book by Steiger!

Office sun rainbow painting with orb

Merkabah

"S"

said, "Oh, my God! I know what this is."

I retrieved Ty's Spirit Book and showed it to Angela. She was amazed. Since that first experience, she has had many soul orbs appear in photos. So have we.

Inside the Merkabah, soul orb, sun boat, interdimensional vehicle of the soul, is the shape of an S. I interpret that as S for sun or soul, maybe for Sher. Also inside the photo is a shape that looks like two rectangles on top of each other.

About two years later, our Japanese exchange student proclaimed to me, "It's a miracle. This looks to me like Japanese kanji, or symbols, for sun."

If you use an online translator from English to Japanese, you will see the similarity:

Sunshine—日照

Sunset—日没

Sunlight—日光

Walking on Sunshine

Japan Merkabah

As related in a previous chapter, one year after Tyler died, our family decided to take a healing trip to Japan to replace our horrid memories with images of the Japan that Ty loved. We planned on meeting our Japanese exchange student and his family, as well as Ty's host family in Japan's Yamanashi prefecture.

One evening after my family had enjoyed a traditional *onsen* hot bath and Japanese-style dinner in Matsumoto, Alec was reclining in a futon mattress on a tatami mat on the floor for bed. I was taking a photo of him and started crying.

Alec asked, "Mom, what's wrong?"

"I miss Ty, Bud. He should be here with us."

Alec said in a matter-of-fact voice, "He is, Mom. Don't you feel him?"

Energy never dies. Alec knew. Alec felt Tyler's energy.

That fall, Alec played hockey. A new friend from his hockey team, Jace, came over to our house for a visit. He had just come from Bible camp and was super-energy-charged. He also shared how he had done a tour of a cemetery in the South and learned about spirit orbs. He said he felt Ty in our home, and also felt like Ty was introducing himself. Alec's friend said he could feel how much fun Ty was.

He and Alec and another friend were jumping on the sofa, frogging around. A most brilliant soul orb shows up in a picture of Jace jumping off the ottoman.

During that time, Allen and I were seeing Christian counselors to protect our marriage. We had been told that eighty to ninety percent of marriages that suffer the death of a child end in divorce. We were trying to beat those odds. So far, so good.

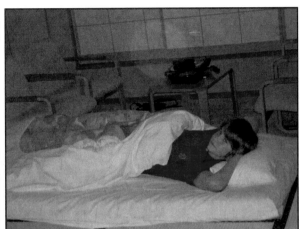

Alec, age 12,
in Japan, with orb

Orb above Jace

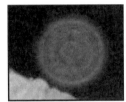

We had male and female pastoral counselors who worked with us for about a year and a half or more, along with a grief counselor, psychologist, who counseled us independently for about the same amount of time. Grief therapy takes time and effort.

I shared the orb phenomenon with my Christian counselors. The male counselor said that I needed to rebuke these orbs and destroy these pictures because they were not in the Bible! I took that as a challenge.

Ezekiel speaks about living creatures with wheels beneath them that sparkle like chrysolite. Chrysolite is a brown or yellow green gemstone symbolic of prudence and wisdom and sometimes disappointed love. Ezekiel describes the wheel as intersecting a wheel. In Jace's orb, there are multiple wheels, giving the appearance of an iris. Ezekiel says that within the wheels were the spirits of the living beings. And the rims of the wheels were full of eyes all around.

If that was not sufficient, John 20:19 and Luke 24:31 proclaim that Christ came through walls and vanished from sight. There are numerous scriptures referring to light, not to mention that the Jewish Kabala references, Merkaveh (Merkabah).

In Atwater's book *The Big Book of Near-Death Experiences*, there are numerous accounts of near-death experiencers seeing light beings. Atwater also writes about the light at the end of the tunnel. I imagine all these glorious souls shine. Their faces are like morning stars. They shine brighter than the sun. Together, they are that light—that light of the Divine Father, Holy Spirit, and Jesus Christ.

In that light, our loved ones shine forever.

Mama

My mother's dementia worsened after Ty's death, so much so that within one and half years, I moved her from Oklahoma to Minnesota and into assisted living. That did not work. Within six months, my mom was in hospice care in our home. She passed away after a few weeks.

Dr. Lermer writes in *Into the Light* that we never die alone. His patients tell him repeatedly that there are many, many angels near them as they pass. They also relive their lives.

I had a baby monitor in my mother's room so that I could hear her from anywhere in my home. My mom also relived the happiest times of her childhood, playing games at a carnival and laughing with me that her arm was so sore from throwing the ball at those cans.

She talked endless hours with my father, who had passed away in 1987. I overheard one conversation: "I know, Art. Isn't it wonderful? I love you, Art. Go on now, I need to rest. I'll see you soon."

Merkabah

And with Jesus, she held her hands up as if grasping something and said, "Oh yes, Lord! Oh thank you! Oh thank you, Jesus!"

I came in and held her other hand with tears in my eyes; she looked at me and said in a very frustrated voice, "Sheryl! Why do you keep doing that? Leave me alone and let me go. Stop bringing me back here!"

Angel Orbs

One evening, near the end of her life, Alec and his friend were in the kitchen playing with the video camera on an Apple computer. They were making some surprised gasps.

I asked what they were doing.

They told me that huge, brilliant orbs were passing around them while they watched. I walked around them to look. I saw them, too. My husband also came into the kitchen.

I had asked caregivers to be with me twenty-four hours a day during my mom's last moments. On that night, it was Comfort (that's really her name). She also saw the orbs. I asked Alec to hit record. We caught the very end of the angel, spirit, soul orb display.

I returned downstairs to my mother's bed. Mom was near death. I was holding vigil. She told me weeks prior, pointing to a chair beside her bed, "I want you right there when I go."

I was trying to create a loving memorial slide show to celebrate her life. Suddenly, the lights in the house flared, and my laptop went off. I looked at my mom. Her eyes darted open, and she exhaled. I held her hand, tearfully whispering, "Is this it, Mom? I love you! Go to the light. Go to Daddy, your one true love. Go to Jesus, Sherry, Joshie, and Ty,

Mom. Go to the many mansions prepared for you. Life is short. I'll see you soon. I love you, Mom. Bless you."

And then she breathed out and left the body that clothed her soul as I kissed her lips for the last time and stroked her silver-gray, curly hair.

Body

Comfort, Mom's hospice-care attendant, and I did for my mom what I could not do for Ty. We bathed her. Washed and curled her hair. I anointed her body with holy water and her feet and forehead with holy oil. We prayed over her.

Then wonderful Wally of Huber Funeral Homes gave up a family vacation and came to collect the body we loved, ever so tenderly, himself. He didn't come in a hearse. He came in a van equipped to carry deceased persons. Mom would've liked that. She hated making a fuss.

That Boy's Spirit

Comfort is from South Africa. She lived with us for the last few weeks of Mom's life. She was pregnant and a university medical student. I am so grateful.

Another nursing aide helping us was from Jamaica. She would relieve Comfort or me during the night so that we could rest. The two of them were talking one evening, when the aide from Jamaica asked, "Do you feel that boy's spirit, Comfort? It feels good."

Comfort told me that she felt very loved in our home and was happy to be with us. We felt loved by her. She was later blessed with a beautiful baby boy. She named her son Tyler. We call him Tee.

Remains

Mom wanted to be cremated. Her ashes were to be placed with my dad in Kasilof, Alaska. My dad had passed away twenty years earlier from lung cancer. Allen, Alec, and I journeyed to Alaska in June with a biodegradable urn filled with my mother's remains.

The Kasilof cemetery is in the middle of a long road not far from the ocean. It's beautiful there. We had to look for mile markers to find the cemetery. The permafrost has left the road lower than the graves. We found the spot the gravedigger made for my mom's ashes, just below my dad's marker. We placed her biodegradable urn in the hole.

We each had a rose. We pulled the buds from the stems, throwing away the thorns as a reminder that Heaven only keeps the good stuff: the bud, fragrance, and essence of our beautiful soul. We placed the petals on Mom's paper urn, covered it with earth, and compressed it lovingly. We said a prayer, *Our Father*, and sang *Amazing Grace*, just the three of us. Mom and Dad have a combined granite marker etched with their favorite couple photo, roses, crosses, and "Together Forever" in the Land of the Midnight Sun.

Rainbows

Alec asked me if I thought Heaven would send us a sign that Grandma Bea made it to Heaven. I told him I hoped so.

As Alec, Allen, and I turned to leave, we were rewarded with a magnificent double-helix rainbow—Heaven's promise of a better tomorrow. The rainbow set the path for us all the way back to our hotel. Alec ran along the Kenai River chasing rainbows. He happened upon a mama moose nursing two calves, a rare sighting.

You made it, Mom! Glory, Mama! Glory Hallelujah!

Angels and Saints

A month before we took Mom's ashes to Alaska, Ty's Japanese host family came to visit us in Minnesota. One day, while sitting around a bonfire, a neighbor asked us about the orbs we saw just before my mom passed. I told him that I believe our loved ones and Heaven's angels and saints are always with us. We simply need to connect with them in faith and love to create the faith-based love and energy field that reaches the realm, making them available to us.

I held up my hand and said, "Heaven's angels and saints, Ty, please be with us in this place. You are welcome here."

Shigemi and Reiko Yajima with spirit orbs

Love Eye in Heaven

Ty's divine transformation happened June of 2007. No matter how much we may try to suppress horrid memories, our subconscious is always aware of past trauma. As time passes, any small trigger can set off an alarm, creating a flood of raw emotions. In the same second, any small trigger can open a flood of healing love that soothes the hurt. Anniversary death dates creep in. Love heals the hurt.

Death Anniversaries

My girlfriends and sisters-in-law booked a lunch and dinner with me on the anniversary of Ty's death in 2010. I was thankful for distractions.

One of my girlfriends, Peggy, shares a birthday on the same date as mine. Four of us met to exchange gifts over lunch and take a leisurely boat cruise on Lake Minnetonka. It's a unique circle. We each knew two of the four of us, but not the third person, until we all came together.

We call ourselves the "Swans and Tigers." Swans represent the soul. Tigers are protectors of the soul. That makes us "Swangers."

Chakra Prayer

The "Swangers" took a boat ride on a sunny day. We were demonstrating a third–eye chakra bowl's healing vibration. We had never had a chakra bowl in our company, so it was a fun and playful prayer date. The bowl's vibrations resonate so strongly, you can actually feel them.

We decided to take communion and pray together. I prayed for a divine distraction to lift my spirit during the anniversary week of Ty's death and funeral. My Swangers united, echoing, "Amen."

I had a leftover supply of communion wafers and cups I had purchased from Kingdom.com (seriously) for our family baptism on the anniversary of Ty's nineteenth birthday.

Mary Beth, one of the four Swangers, asked me if she could have four communions and the third–eye chakra singing bowl to take to another group of her friends. Mary Beth has an amazing voice and is a cantor in her Catholic church. One of her friends is also a cantor. Mary Beth's cantor friend was diagnosed with terminal cancer.

It's hard for me to write those words because I believe that our thoughts can become negative prayers. So let me say, Mary Beth has a friend who is recovering from cancer unless her soul is ready. Mary Beth wanted to recreate the blessing we felt with the chakra bowl and communion. Mary Beth had also proclaimed that day that she felt a fundraiser coming into our lives.

Love Eye in Heaven

Stop

After the Swangers' lunch and boat ride, I was on my way to join my sisters-in-law for dinner. There was a traffic jam on a county road that passes by Resurrection Cemetery where Ty's sunshine castle harbors the remains of the body that clothed his soul. The stoplight was blinking red. I was humbled and awestruck that an unlikely traffic light malfunction would jam traffic as my car was parallel to Ty's crypt on the anniversary of the day his heart stopped. I blew a kiss and promised to stop on my way home because his aunts were waiting for me, tears included.

Surprise

My cell phone rang while I was detained in traffic. It was Twin Cities Live (TCL) calling to tell me that my personal trainer, Stacy Clark of Tiger Athletics, had nominated me for TCL's Slim Down Makeover. They asked if I would be interested in showcasing my success on Channel 5 within a week!

Stacy had told them that my son and my mother had died within two years of each other and that I was making my health and myself priorities by working out. I had lost twenty-five pounds.

Prayers answered! I was about to be distracted in a very positive way for seven to ten days. I phoned Mary Beth to tell her my exciting news. She did not answer, so I left a voice mail message. As soon as my phone call ended, the stoplight began working again, and traffic was back to normal. I thanked Heaven, my girlfriends, and Tyler for the miraculous distraction and timing.

Each Knew Two

arrived a few minutes late for dinner because of the stoplight stuck on red. The anniversary of Ty's death is devastating for our entire family. Candy was with my son, Alec, in Chicago on that day. She and Alec have a bond that only people who have been together in tragedy can have. She and Alec went back to Chicago a year later to replace sad memories with happier ones. I was very happy to be with my sisters-in-law, Candy and Minda, and share my exciting news on this anniversary date.

As we enjoyed our wine. Mary Beth phoned me back, ecstatic. It was a brief conversation, but she wanted to tell me how incredible it was to have the singing bowl and communion with her friends. My sisters-in-law overheard my conversation.

When I hung up, Minda said, "Sheryl, you have a friend who is a cantor in a Catholic church who is diagnosed with terminal cancer?" I explained it was the friend of my friend. To be brief, it was revealed that night that this friend is also a friend of my sister-in-law. I called Mary Beth back to confirm.

I knew Mary Beth and Minda. Minda knew me and Mary Beth's friend. Mary Beth knew me and her cantor friend. We each knew two out of three, but not the third. It happens to us all the time.

We invited Mary Beth to join us for dinner because the occurrences were surreal for all of us, goose bumps included.

As we were dining, Candy mentioned that she desperately wanted to build a sunshine healing garden for physical therapy at Gillette's Children Hospital. The sunshine fundraiser was revealed. What a day!

Love Eye in Heaven

I was driving Ty's Kia that night. The keys to his Sunshine Castle were in my car, not in the Kia, so I wouldn't be able to open the door to the mausoleum. On my way home, I stopped at the cemetery anyway. Ample moonlight shone through the skylights and stained glass sun murals near the ceiling. I could see Ty's granite, sealed with *Walking on Sunshine*.

I touched my forehead to the glass and whispered to him, "I love you, Buddy. I will always love you. Thank you for today! I know you love me back. Life is short. I'll see you soon! Thanks for choosing me. I am so proud to be your Momsy. I'm loving Dad and Alec. I'll see you soon. Life is short."

Throughout the next week, the anniversary week of Ty's death and funeral, I was busy filming my segments, trying on outfits, getting my hair and makeup revamped, and appearing on television with my close friends, husband, and son. It was a very happy time.

Love Eye

That year, Abbey, Ty's girlfriend, was studying in Europe the same week of Tyler's death and funeral anniversary. Like me, the memory of being with Ty when the respirator was removed is traumatic. It's an agonizing and painful memory. Abbey and I try to talk and work through it together, combining our prayers for powerful solutions to love and honor Tyler while we move on with our lives.

Ty often called Abbey his goddess. She studied photography and journalism at Iowa State, and graduated in 2012. She loves to travel. She has been to Australia, Israel, Japan, Spain, England, Guyana, and a number of other places. She has literally taken thousands and thousands of photos in her travels. Until Ty's death, she never had Merkabah appear in them. They do now. Merkabah are with her in high-energy photo shots.

Abbey and I sometimes chat on the Internet. We remain very close friends. Abbey was telling me how much she dreaded the coming week and the anxiety it brought. We talked about anger and grief and remorse. I asked her to try and celebrate Ty's life by doing something happy on his angel day, sharing the love with others. I would try to do the same. Life goes on.

The next day, I went shopping for some pampering items to mail to her. I bought lavender scents, inspirational note cards, and candles. I mailed them off. It was as much healing for me to send Abbey a love package as I hope it was for her to receive it.

I also started an acrylic painting of a beautiful peacock for Abbey, with solar feathers and a white heart in its pupil. I call it *Love Eye in Heaven*. As I painted the peacock, Abbey was touring France.

Love Eye in Heaven
peacock painted for Abbey

She told me she was going to go to the Eiffel Tower and hoped to meet the man of her dreams. She posted a photo of herself on Facebook next to a statue of an elephant that was painted in peacock feathers. She also posted photos of herself at the Eiffel Tower. In the Eiffel Tower photo of her, there are numerous Merkabah. Bright, vibrant ones! In the upper right, one particularly large Merkabah looks like an eye.

Love Eye in Heaven

Abbey in Paris, surrounded by Merkabah, with close-up of the "love eye in heaven"

Tyler is ever present in our minds and hearts on the anniversary of his transformation. These Merkabah bring me peace and hope for a life eternal in love and light. They are beautiful and awe-inspiring to me, especially since I saw their motion, color, and energy with my mom's passing away.

I believe the man of Abbey's dreams showed up that night because she was remembering him. I hope she finds true love in her remaining days on earth. A guardian angel is watching over her.

It has been my experience that messages can appear in Merkabah, like the S and Japanese kanji for sun in the Merkabah of the photo of the sun rainbow. In two, Angela and I have seen smiley faces. Angela told me that she sees two people in the lower left of the love eye Merkabah. Others have told me they see three.

We have come to understand that we can call orbs into our presence by sending love out to the universe. Hold someone in your heart who is in the light. The Merkabah appear.

Medium

Sylvie, our French exchange student, is now happily married, with two three-year-old boys. They came to visit us in summer of 2010. My niece was also visiting with her husband.

Sylvie, along with my niece and I, had planned to go to a makeover studio and have a ladies' night out, getting our hair and makeup done. That didn't work out. On arrival, we learned that our appointments were cancelled because our stylist had been in an auto accident.

Sylvie asked if we could go visit Tyler's crypt instead. Sylvie had been eight months pregnant, in the hospital, protecting her twins during Tyler's funeral. She loved Ty, but could not come.

Sylvie's babies were born healthy and happy on Bastille Day, July 14, the day France became a modern nation. Ty would have loved that with his passion for history. The boys came a few weeks early.

Love Eye in Heaven

Timing

I had the key to the mausoleum in my car, so we agreed to go visit Ty's resting place. My niece's birthday is June 29, the day Tyler was removed from the respirator. Her husband's birthday is also July 5, the day we held Ty's memorial. They could not come to his memorial service either. They had just married.

Seeing Ty's resting place was a reality-shock finale for all of us. We held each other, extending one hand to Ty's granite marker while saying *Our Father* and a prayer, telling Tyler we loved him. The sun made rainbow prisms dance around us through the stained glass windows.

We arrived home to tell our husbands about our change of plans. We lit a candle, prayed together, and shared communion. We decided to take a boat ride out on the lake. Fluffy clouds dotted the sky. We looked toward the sun, loving Tyler, being thankful for each other, when a rainbow halo appeared around the sun, again. It was glorious! Like a little touch of the divine reminding us that we are loved eternally.

Sylvie named her boys Theo and Alex, coincidentally similar to Ty and Alec. Later in the evening,

Fluffy cloud with halo and rainbow around the sun

we watched our international grandsons while their mom and dad and American second cousins went on a moonlight boat cruise together. The boys call us Mama Sherille and Papa Allen.

SOL Boat

Ty used to putter around in a 1959 Cutter boat that had belonged to his paternal grandpa. He took a lot of pride in the fact that his grandpa trusted him. In Wisconsin, you can drive a motor boat at the age of twelve when accompanied by an adult. Ty would spend endless hours cruising circles on the lake. His grandpa told him he could have

Ty's SOL boat

that boat when he was gone because he enjoyed it and loved it so much. It gave us all a lot of pleasure to see how much happiness Tyler enjoyed driving the cutter.

After Tyler died, Grandpa told us we could come get it. We took the boat Ty loved to drive and had it restored. It is a very cute, small boat that seats four comfortably. It has classic wings on the rear and a large steering wheel. We named the boat *SOL*—SOL for sun and because it sounds like soul. Ty's SOuL boat brought tears to Grandma and Grandpa's eyes and ours. We often take a sunset cruise in Ty's SOuL boat, sending out love on sun and moon beams all the way to paradise and eternity. We are grateful.

Mama Sherille

Allen and I took Theo and Alex onto a porch swing, one on each of our laps. These two three-year-old boys could only speak French. They weren't too happy that Mama and Papa left them with us to cruise the lake with our niece and nephew. We knew a few French words to communicate with them. Love is an international language. They cuddled down with their blankies and waited, Theo in Allen's lap and Alex in mine.

We rocked back and forth, looking at the moon's reflection on the lake. I was reminiscing about Ty and Alec in our early family with Sylvie, and this next generation. My nephew took a photo of our home from the bay. There, on the horizon, as big as a moon, is a faint but evident Merkabah above the four of us on the swing, Allen, Theo, Alex, and me. Feel the love.

Sun Signals

I've had other miraculous sun signals with surreal timing.

The first December after Ty's death, I received a phone call from Abbey, checking in to see how we were doing. I told her my house was so quiet. I did not have teenage-boy voices bellowing from downstairs for snacks. My house did not vibrate with the same energy. It was too quiet, less fun.

She suggested we have a party. I loved that idea. We invited kids who were on Ty's trip to Japan to a cookie decorating and eating party.

What great fun! The big boys arrived with their high energy, and instantly, my house felt like home again. They surrounded each other in brotherly hugs in the foyer. Some of the girls came too and livened things up by dominating electronic games. I took a photo. One Merkabah was on them and one on the wall. The one on the wall had a smiley face in it.

We decorated gingerbread houses and cookies, played electronic games and board games. We talked about upcoming plans for graduation and colleges. Some of the kids wanted to go into Ty's room and pick out a keepsake.

Sun Signals

Concern

The kids told me they had recently seen one of the leaders on the Japan tour and were worried about him. They asked me to call to try and help. Me. They asked me, Tyler's mom. I told them I would see what I could do.

It was a big request. In Japan, the leaders went home with the student tour group while we stayed behind, preparing to disconnect Tyler from the respirator. The kids would not know that Ty had died until they returned and were with families. I had not spoken to any of the leaders since. We were preparing for Tyler's wrongful death lawsuit. Not the best environment for a chat.

I did try to call one morning. Voice mail picked up. I put my head down on my desk and sobbed relief. I spoke out loud, "If it was really meant for me to phone, there would have been a person answering."

Sun tower

Walking on Sunshine

I picked up my head, wiped my eyes, and looked out the window. The sunrise had just crested the horizon. A sun tower shot up from the sun to infinity. It was the second sun tower I had ever seen. The first one was on our first Thanksgiving without Tyler at his Aunt Candy's house, at sunset. I have not seen one since.

I took the sun tower as a message from Heaven to try again. The second time I phoned, the call was answered. Odd how divine providence works.

Trinity Sun

A year later, I was scheduled to be deposed by defense attorneys in Tyler's wrongful death lawsuit. I woke up before sunrise to get in a workout. I went into my office with a cup of coffee to relax, meditate, and collect myself. I wanted to honor Tyler with grace and grit. In my meditation, I imagined the holy trinity embracing me in light. When I opened my eyes, this was the sunrise I saw:

Trinity sunrise

Sun Signals

I was in such awe of the beauty of this sunrise that time seemed to stand still. My breath was taken away in admiration of the magnificent trinity of light. The rainbow effect of the light was on both sides.

Years later, I am still amazed. This is the screensaver on my cell phone, divine light. These are called sun dogs; I call them trinity lights.

At a counseling session shortly afterward, I shared the photo and experience. One pastor asked if I really believed that God would shine that sun just for me because many people must have seen it.

My answer, I do. I really do. I believe divine love can make a connection that transcends time and distance. I believe that sunrise touched the hearts of many, many people. And like me, they are grateful and blessed. It is unforgettable.

It's like Ty told us when he was five, "When you have a blessing, you have to share it."

I hope many people share glorious sun moments and ponder the magnificence of our universe. Be blessed. Be the blessing.

Sun Halo

My Swanger girlfriends met with me for an early lunch on a warm spring day. We were sitting outside. I had brought some small inspirational gifts to share and a bouquet of daisies. Mary Beth accidentally knocked the daisies off the table and every last blossom broke off the stem. We laughed about the odds of that happening. Daisies signify innocence and gentleness, devoid of sin or guilt, and being adaptable. We laughed as we thought about the significance of the daisies tumble.

Walking on Sunshine

Mary Beth had asked us to pray for her daughter because she was applying for a highly competitive internship during the summer.

I said, "I'd rather thank Heaven that she has the job."

Mary Beth laughed.

I said, "No really, Mary Beth. She's got the job. I know she's got the job. You are going to contact us this afternoon after she confirms she got the job."

Mary Beth laughed again, tossing her head back, and then said, "Oh, my God! Look! Look at the sun!"

Sun halo

We did. There was a vibrant rainbow halo around the entire sun. None of us had a camera. I took a photo with my cell phone. It was about 11:30 a.m. on a cloudless day, June 3, springtime in Minnesota. Humidity was practically zero.

Mary Beth texted us at about three o'clock that afternoon to confirm that her daughter had indeed gotten the job.

Sun Signals

Serendipity! It is fun to make fortunate discoveries. I cannot explain how I knew that Mary Beth's daughter had already gotten the job. I just did.

Spiritual Gifts

Atwater, in *The Big Book of Near-Death Experiences*, explains how special gifts are rewarded to people who have seen the light and return. Intelligence, psychic abilities, artistic talents, and more have been documented.

There is speculation that Einstein and Edison were near-death experiencers. I've read tales about how they would quiet their mind to resolve a problem, nod off placing a pencil or a cup on their head, wake up when it rolled off, and write down first thoughts, often solutions.

Spiritual Power

I have a dear friend who calls me a glorious soul. My prayers are so powerful. We are all glorious souls with powerful prayers. All too often, I believe that we pray, not believing. Or our prayers are selfishly self-centered. We pray to be thin and healthy, but our self-image is fat and unhealthy. Which one wins depends on the desire of your heart. I believe we must visualize the change we want to see, and that it must be a greater good for a greater whole, based on love. If we cannot visualize our belief, how can it manifest? I think we must reach for it, grasp it, and be grateful.

Walking on Sunshine

I have learned to meditate, to be still, to listen to the divine. The answers come. It's hard for Heaven to reach us when our thoughts are so noisy. We interfere. We aren't tuning in.

Through grief and despair, I bottomed out with total emptiness. I often wonder if it was then that Heaven filled my emptiness with divine love, a touch from Heaven, grace.

I have come to know Christ Consciousness. I desire it. To meditate in a way that elevates one's soul. The meditation ends, then it is back to real life, with renewed energy and wisdom.

I interpret Gnostic texts to define Christ consciousness as a bridal chamber, a place where interaction—connectedness—with Christ makes us one in him, much like communion.

To a Parent

I am coming to understand that our children, alive in the light, cannot reach us when we are smothered in grief. It's like a fog so thick, light cannot penetrate it. There is no grief or despair in Heaven.

We must grieve. We must all have our Good Friday before our Easter Sunday. Scripture gave those mourning for Moses a time to put away their grief. Give permission and time to unfold from grief and reach for the light.

I still grieve. There are heartache moments when my steel resolve melts under the intense energy of love I feel. Tears cascade, blessed tears, washing away the pain. And then I breathe in a holy breath and thank Heaven that I know love that transcends time. I hold Tyler and my loved ones up. I hold you up! In my heart, I visualize their ever-expanding living souls. It helps me overcome anxiety to emanate my love in a healing light of powerful intent to the souls I love in eternity. Every single loving thought penetrates and reaches them and expands my own soul.

Good Friday is over! It's Easter Sunday! Peace be with you.

My Glorious Sons

People ask me about my children. I tell them I have two sons, Tyler, who passed away in 2007, and Alec. I will always be Tyler and Alec's mom for all eternity. No one can take that from me. I am blessed. Alec will always have a big brother for all eternity. No one can take that from him.

I cringe when faces hollow and expected murmurs release "I'm so sorry."

I have come to say, "Bless Ty's glorious soul."

It was hard to walk out in public after Ty's death. People would look at me and start crying. I started sending out advance notices, "I'm coming to school. Smile when you see me. It lifts me up."

Every year, secret friends put angels in my mailbox, love notes on my door, plaques on my steps, sunflowers near Tyler's earthly remains, and ribbons on his memorial trees. I appreciate these special gifts of remembrance from secret friends.

Walking on Sunshine

Alec is absolutely super, not that he didn't have his angry, sad times, too. But here he is. He is on a track for success and studies with intent. He makes good choices. He honors his brother with his life, which in turn honors us.

At this writing, Alec is now living the eighteenth year of his life as a high school senior. He looks more like his dad every day. He is tall and lanky, unlike Ty's husky self. He is in his last year of school. We all get that. On April 1, 2011, Alec had outlived his brother.

Alec has a unique sense of humor, a nerdy intense intelligence, and is a gifted writer and artist. He also has a tender heart. He likes hanging out with friends, music, wakeboarding, lacrosse, and playing goalie in hockey. He wants to travel the world and protect our oceans. Yay! Shine, Buddy! Shine!

Chariot of Spirit

I am paying attention. I seek the Spirit, the real self, their glorious souls, the ones we love. They do not wear the raiment of their earthly bodies. They were carried to eternity in a chariot of spirit. Enjoy the journey.

Enjoy the journey! Love each other. Grow your soul. It's okay if we're not perfect.

We live forever in eternity, in eternal light, the everlasting Sun, NRG, transformed by Love. Our light shines forever in the next place that we go.

Wonder

I recently created a LinkedIn profile. It's been great fun connecting with my healthcare account team from US West, prior clients, and technical support. Social media can help you reconnect with people you haven't seen for decades. One US West coworker, Barb, and I got together for lunch for the first time in years.

She told me about the death of her father and about a seer whose last name is bizarrely similar to Wonder. Ms. Wondra is also an information technology executive. Barb told me how Ms. Wondra felt her father's presence and relayed messages her dad had for her. She told me her dad had been tough on her and somehow, she had always managed to disappoint him. Ms. Wondra told her that her dad wanted to apologize for ridiculing her and that he was very proud of her. She also said her dad was surrounded by three wives. Barb's dad had been widowed three times. There is no jealousy in Heaven. I wonder if wives who did not know each other on earth see each other in Heaven.

I let Barb see my sun photo. We talked for hours about Merkabah, intuitive feelings, and other wonderful connections that let us know our loved ones are here even after they've passed. Barb suggested that Ms. Wondra and I should meet. She set up a coffee date for us a few days out.

Walking on Sunshine

Get Back Up

The morning of our luncheon, I was looking for a Spanish dictionary in Tyler's bookcase. I found a book Ty had written in elementary school titled *I Like Me*. There was a photo of Ty after he had fallen off his bike. The caption read, "When I fall, I get back up."

Ms. Wondra and I met for coffee. She said that all morning, she had had an image of Tyler on a bike as a young boy, but that felt really strange, because she knew he was sixteen years old when he died. I told her about *I Like Me*. We both agreed Tyler must be telling me, "Get back up."

We talked about psychic interventions and how wonderfully strange they can feel. She told me that she keeps hearing "goddess" around me, over and over.

"It's like you are a goddess," Ms. Wondra said.

I smiled knowingly and looked up. I held out my arms and replied, "I receive."

Ms. Wondra then said that she needed to give me a stone. An image of this stone was repeatedly in her thoughts that morning. She said it was like Tyler really wanted me to have this one and no other. From her pocket, she took a rose quartz stone that had been lovingly shaped and polished into a heart. My breath seized. I excused myself and went to the restroom, where my sobs became a joyful reunion with my Tyler's love.

Wonder

Lovesy Goddess Momsy

Tyler used to wake up in the morning and come to me with puppy eyes and ask, "Lovesy Goddess Momsy, would you make me a love breakfast?" A love breakfast was a breakfast I would make personally, just for him, like buttermilk biscuits with sausage patties, eggs, and cheddar cheese. Ty could eat three with hash browns and orange juice. Or I would make chocolate chip pancakes—really big ones.

When Ty's Minnetonka Moose U16 hockey team players drop by to big brother Alec or give me big-boy love, they sometimes spend the night. I make my "Lovesy Goddess Momsy" love breakfast for them as well. It's very therapeutic.

Stone Hearts

When Ty was five years old and Alec one, I was working long hours. I was called away to present at a health informatics symposium in Park City, Utah. I decided to take Caroline from Sweden and my boys with me because I missed them so much.

I had a fun evening, riding down the bobsled track at Park City with Ty. There was a porcupine on the track near the bottom, directly in front of us. We couldn't stop. We couldn't slow down. We hit it at full speed. It bounced up, landed on all four feet, shook itself off, and walked away. Ty said, "Wow, Mom! What an adventure! I can't wait to tell my friends!"

Walking on Sunshine

Later we went to dinner and then dessert at the Chocolate Factory. A visit to the Chocolate Factory has become a family tradition every time we visit Park City. Caroline wanted to shop around a bit, and so we did. Ty came to me in a store and told me he needed five dollars to buy a gift for me. I asked what. But he told me it was a surprise. He stuffed something about the size of the palm of my hand into his little pocket.

That evening during bedtime stories, Ty brought out his present. A big, heart–shaped granite stone, polished smooth.

Ty looked at me with love eyes and said, "Do you get it, Mom? This is my love for you. It's like a stone. It lasts forever." Ty was always giving me stone hearts to express his love for me. I have many.

Now I have one more made of rose quartz. Rose quartz symbolizes love. One more—a stone love heart. Ooh aah!

Tyler's name means "foundation builder" or "brick layer" in Celtic. His name also means "stone."

Big Plans

I told Ms. Wondra through love-filled, teary eyes about the goddess and love that lasts forever in stone hearts. She told me that she sees me traveling and speaking and making a big difference in the divine plan.

Before he went to Japan, Tyler told me God had a big plan for me. Let the love begin.

YeM!

This book is an act of love and courage. I continue to experience divine energy. I hope to for all eternity.

One night, as I was nearing the completion of *Walking on Sunshine*, I was in that alpha state between sleep and wakefulness and felt Ty brushing my hair.

He was looking deeply into my eyes with so much love, repeating, "YeM, Mom! YeM!"

I said, "I don't understand YeM, Buddy."

He said, "Remember YeM, Mom! Please remember YeM!"

I said, "Okay, Darling, I'll remember YeM."

I lifted myself out of bed, walked to my home office, and wrote down the word "YeM," then went back to sleep.

The following morning, I Googled, "Define YeM."

YeM is the name of a Hebrew girl. The meaning of the name is "Life."

Perhaps that is my Heavenly name. Life.

Perhaps that is my message from Tyler, "Remember life, Mom. We live forever."

Walking on Sunshine

Your Story

I've been encouraged to write a second book about similar experiences from other persons. If you have a story you would like to submit, please visit my author website at www.walkingonsunshine.org.

Feel the love that's really real.

Afterword

The number-one reason most of us want a connection with our loved ones who have "passed" is to know they are well and that it's all good. It's remarkably hard to soothe grief without this connection—and remarkably easy when the connection is made.

Every ending is a new beginning. A glorious transformation, like the opening of a water lily. Our next life is a symbol of all that is true, good and beautiful, blessed with peace, love, and enlightenment.

So how do you make this connection?

- **Intent:** Talk to them. Journal, write letters, poems, get your thoughts and feelings down. Put intent into your writing.

- **Flip the Switch:** When we are shrouded in a fog of grief so thick that light cannot penetrate, our loved ones cannot reach us. Every day you live, you are closer to where they are. Life is terminal; we all die. It is how we choose to live that grows our soul, celebrates life and our loved ones who have passed. Raise them up with your remembrances. You can do it. Life is short, a blink in eternity.

♥ **Relax:** Light a candle in remembrance. Use aroma therapy, like lavender or chamomile. Play soft, comforting music.

♥ **Energy:** Get grounded. Our bodies resonate at 60-120 Hz. Energy cannot be created or destroyed, only transformed. Energy is felt and transformed in static shocks. Defibrillators restart heartbeats. Release negative energy down to the earth. Throw it down. The earth loves gravity; it's a gift.

♥ **Breathe:** Replace negative energy with a holy breath. Breathe deeply and exhale an "ocean" breath (deep sigh). Close your eyes to block out external stimulation.

♥ **Visualize:** Imagine that divine light is entering your soul with every breath, connecting you with paradise and your loved one. Reach for it; it's coming to you. Embrace it. Let your heart overflow with divine love for the person who is transformed.

♥ **Listen:** When our minds are so noisy with thoughts, we cannot hear our loved ones. Quiet your mind. Relax, breathe deeply, and pay attention.

♥ **Pay Attention:** You might feel a tingle, twitches, or tiny electric pulses that make the hair on your skin rise up. You might hear a hush, vibration, or tone in your ear. You may feel warm or hot. In your mind's eye, you might see colors or light. Go with it. The deeper we are in mediation, the better we feel and the stronger the connection.

♥ **Light:** Like fiber optics, light carries transmissions. Tune into the messages you are receiving. Consciously connect with the light.

♥ **Return:** Open your eyes. Rub your hands and face. It may take a moment for you to feel fully awake. Write down your experience.

Afterword

- **Be Grateful**: Acknowledge this sacred time. Love, remember, and cherish your loved ones. Be grateful for their presence in your life.

- **Synchronicity:** Look for signs of your loved ones. Many people who have been introduced to "orbs" —also known as Merkahbah or soul light bodies, begin to see them in their own lives. Welcome them during celebrations. Keep a journal of signs from your loved ones.

What if you can't make the connection?

- **Get Help:** very much like placing a call in a Third World country, you may need to use a third-party professional operator for help.

- **Licensed Psychologists** are using EMDR (Eye Movement Desensitization Reprocessing) to Instigate After-Death Communications (IADC) or Guided Afterlife Connections (GAC). Reports are being published that demonstrate how IADC and GAC soothe grief, helping our soldiers and persons who have been traumatized by death normalize and live healthier lives.

  EMDR is an approved therapy for post-traumatic stress disorder. Many patients have experienced IADCs or GACs with licensed psychologists using EMDR therapies. *Walking on Sunshine* is one example. Another bold telling is *The Reason* by Salley Grablick, whose son died from suicide. Suicides are particularly difficult and painful. Connections with those who have died through suicide are very healing.

- ♥ **Licensed Mediums:** Most people are reluctant to trust mediums. They can cost hundreds or even thousands of dollars with no guarantee that the person you want to connect with will respond. Authentic mediums are often passed over because of poor performers. Windbridge Certified Research Mediums strive to validate professionals. Troy Parkinson, Minnesota, is a certified medium through Windbridge, film maker, and author of *Bridge to the Afterlife.*

- ♥ **Religion:** Author Sally Grablick states, "Religion is for people who believe in Hell. Spirituality is for those who have been there." Death, like birth, is painful. The next place we go is bright, joyful, and loving. Give yourself permission. Books like *Heaven is Real* affirm that our loved ones exist after death. People of all religions connect with their loved ones in the light. You would not be the first religious person to heal this way.

- ♥ The **International Association for Near-Death Studies** (IANDS) researches life-after-death experiences if you want to learn from people who have died and come back to life.

- ♥ **Courage:** Share your experiences so others will know that love never dies. Our loved ones live forever. Life and love are eternal.

- ♥ Your **rewards** are promise, hope, love, and the absence of fear. These make the journey of life worth celebrating. Grow your soul in light and love.

Namaste … may our light shine together in the next place we go: Oneness.

References & Resources

(listed alphabetically)

After Death Communication Research Foundation: www.adcrf.org/

Apocryphon of John: www.gnosis.org

Atwater, P.M.H. *The Big Book of Near-Death Experiences,*
www.cinemind.com

Bereavement Support: www.dragonflyproject.org

Christofferson, B.J., Sun Shrine Artist: www.bjchristofferson.com

Consciousness, Forums, Life after Death: youreternalself.com/

Depart Smart: Safe Travel Starts Here: www.departsmart.org.
Follow us on Twitter, Facebook and LinkedIn
Travel consumer protection is sorely missing in a $7+ trillion travel and
tourism industry. There are no warnings before you buy or fly. Depart
Smart provides tools to help you identify and mitigate risks, get help and
get home. The only surprises should be good ones.

Hanson, Warren, *The Next Place*: www.warrenhanson.com

Howorka, Dr. Kinga, Functional Insulin Treatment: www.diabetesfit.org

Induced After Death Communication using EMDR by Licensed
Psychologists: www.induced-adc.com/

International Association of Near Death Studies: www.iands.org
www.afterdeathconference.org, Affirming the continuity of life, love and
communication after death

Kimmie Rose is an internationally renowned medium with CBS Sky Radio-
Inner Views: www.kimmierose.com/

Lerma, Dr. John, *Into the Light*: www.drjohnlerma.com

Morningstar, Molly, evidential psychic medium, www.mollymorningstar.com

Parkinson, Troy, Windbridge Certified Research Medium, Minnesota
www.troyparkinson.com

Sloat, John W., Spiritual Awakening (former minister for 40 years):
www.beyondreligion.com

Spring Forest Qi Gong with Master Lin: www.springforestqigong.com

Stephens, Necole, spirit medium, Reiki Master, hypnotist, nonprofit founder
(& bereaved mother): www.necolestephens.com

Support Group for Parents of Deceased Children:
www.compassionatefriends.org

Tyler Hill's Story: www.tylerhill.org

Ty's Spirit Book: *Real Ghosts, Restless Spirits & Haunted Places*,
www.bradandsherry.com/

Wright, Rochelle, Grief counseling & guided after–death communications
with EMDR: www.rochellewright.com/

About the Author

S heryl Hill is a world speaker, award-winning author, and artist. Her professional career centered on information technology and communications for health-care major markets working for fortune 500 companies. She and her family founded Depart Smart dba ClearCause Foundation in 2010 after years of advocating for student travel safety. Depart Smart has influenced student abroad transparency laws.

To reach Sheryl Hill, please send an email through www.departsmart.org or www.walkingonsunshing.org. You can also find her on Twitter, SherylDHill, or LinkedIn.

Note: On December 31, 2015, People to People Student Ambassadors went out of business.

Depart Smart
Safe travel starts here

All over the world, tourism protection is poor.
People just go, under-insured and under-prepared.

Depart Smart provides online, consumer-driven travel safety tools to develop life-saving skills for safe journeys.

A small fee can save your life and the lives of people you love.

Our priorities:

- Awareness
- Travel Safety Tools for Safe Journeys and Emergency Preparedness
- Advocacy

The only surprises should be the good ones. We love happy endings. Please give at www.DepartSmart.org. Be the light.